Marianne Larned
2011

Blessed Among Women

By Arnold Michael, D.D., L.H.D.

2002
Global Citizen Publishing
San Clemente, California

Published by
Global Citizen Publishing
San Clemente, California

Copyright, 1948
By Arnold Michael
Revised Second Printing, 1971
Third Printing, 1973
Fourth Printing, 1978
Fifth Printing, 1980
Revised Edition, 1986
Revised Edition, 2002
Copyright transfer to Charles Sommer, 2002

Printed in the United States of America
By
Lightning Source Inc.
La Vergne, TN 37086

Blessed Among Women is dedicated to Emily Kay, my wife, my friend, my co-worker, and my unconditional love. Her every thought, word, and deed confirms the following statement by Goethe: The Eternal Feminine draws us upward.

The Magnificat

And Mary said, *"My soul magnifies the Lord, and my spirit rejoices in God my Savior; For he has regarded the meekness of his handmaid: for behold, from henceforth, all generation shall bless me."* Luke 1, 46-48

Blessed Among Women has touched the hearts of thousands of readers and has prompted us to grow in the awareness the Divine Presence.

It is through meekness that we discover Essential Divinity. For if God dwells in any of us, He/She/It dwells in all of us.

God is Love.

The ultimate sacrifice is to give up that which separates us from our Essential Divinity. We can never kill Essential Divinity. It yearns to be discovered within us.

Thank you Mother Mary for being an example of that discovery. And thank you Arnold Michael for your vivid portrayal of Her.

Charles Sommer—Co Director of the Madonna Ministry,
(The organization founded by Arnold Michael)

FOREWORD

I have twice read *Blessed Among Women*. The first reading was in manuscript. The second was in galley proof. This gave me the rare experience of finding the second reading more delightful than the first. Usually, after a book has been read once, most of the bloom is rubbed off by familiarity. But with this book, the rule does not hold. I am looking forward to the third reading in book form, and I anticipate an even greater treat.

There is something unique and original in this story, both in treatment and material. It is a book rather difficult to classify, although the author is obviously a novelist. The book is a novel and yet it reads like a composite biography of the world's greatest two women: the mother of God's Son and the mother of John, the Baptist. These famous women are treated with extraordinary perception, delicate understanding and sympathy. The story has the sweep also of a great allegory and the lingering power of a legend.

The author has done his work well, for it seems at times almost as though he were *written through*, so smoothly does the narrative flow.

The best thing about the book I can say is simply this, I wish I had written it.

The author has not been handicapped by any outworn creeds and sterile theological half-truths. He writes with a freedom that borders well-nigh on license at times and this gives the reader a long breath of freshness after wading through the endless run of religious books. Though this is a religious book, it is not a preachy, pious book. Arnold Michael has written with a genuinely spiritual dare which few authors have the courage to attempt.

I wish for it a warm public reception. It deserves a wide circulation. I am quite sure that no reader will be disappointed. I believe that each reader will both want to keep the book and pass it on to a friend. It is the kind of book people read and talk about and wrap for a gift.

Starr Daily

Starr Daily was a hardened criminal who spent fourteen years in penitentiaries and chain gangs. He had a Road to Damascus enlightening experience, much like Saul who became St. Paul. Starr's life dramatically changed and he became the catalyst for change in the penal system, stimulated prison reforms, obtained an early release and became best known for his lectures and his first book entitled "Love Can Open Prison Doors." Glenn Clark wrote his spiritual biography entitled "From Crime to Christ" in 1948.

THE GENESIS OF
BLESSED AMONG WOMEN

During World War II, I operated the dining room of Hotel Laguna in Laguna Beach, California. The surf came within a few feet of the dining room and late at night when it was quiet in the hotel, I would stroll along the beach and sit on a bench to look at the heavens and listen to the gentle surf.

One night a stranger joined me on the beach. He had a small booklet in his hand and began talking about it. He said it was written by a Jewess from Palestine who, a few years before, had lectured in this country on its contents.

The book dealt with the history of the various tribes or branches of the House of David during the time of Jesus. The author of the booklet was Lydia M. Mountford. She was a member of that branch of the House of David whose responsibility it was to perpetuate the history of all the branches since the time of David himself.

There was no Bible and very few books in those days, so *word of mouth* had to be used as the means of perpetuation, similar to the perpetuation of Free Masonry. This necessitated a continuous sequence of generations within the family to *carry on* the historical information. Lydia M. Mountford was the only member of the last generation and that is why she decided to print this information concerning the Holy Family.

The stranger presented me with the booklet stating that

I would find it very meaningful. Then he departed. I never saw him again.

I did not realize I was particularly interested in the Holy Family until the booklet revealed that at the time of Jesus, the Holy Family was similar to the Royal Family of England in the sense that the various members were of great wealth, culture, and refinement.

Mary's father was a Persian prince and her mother a princess of the House of David. Through their marriage, the Magi and the Jews were united. Joseph was prince of that branch of the House of David called the Carpenter Tribe because for generations they were the designers and builders of synagogues.

Elizabeth, the mother of John the Harbinger, was also of nobility. Against this background of culture, nobility, and refinement, Mary and Elizabeth shared the privilege and responsibility of giving birth to and rearing the Messiah and his Messenger. I say *shared* because they were cousins and very close.

This royalty of the Holy Family thrilled me with its appropriateness. I felt that was as it should be! I carefully read the New Testament to determine the source of the concept of poverty. The one and only reference in the Bible to the material circumstances of the Holy Family was the statement that Joseph was a carpenter. During those days, everyone knew he was Prince of the Carpenter Tribe!

The statement of the stranger that this different concept of the Holy Family would be meaningful to me was a great understatement. It became the most meaningful thing in my life. The compulsion to share this truth with others was so undeniably compelling that I had to leave my busi-

iv

ness for six months to write a book about it.

When it was finished, I sent it to several publishers who rejected it. So I ceased my efforts and returned my full interest to my business.

Then another stranger appeared in my life. I did not hear of him until after he had read the manuscript and influenced a publisher to publish it. He was Starr Daily, who provided the foreword of this book. Later, another stranger in Mexico City wrote for permission to publish it in Spanish!

Blessed Among Women, I believe, is an entity capable of fulfilling its own purpose, which is to portray how the human personality, by expressing unconditional love, can become the chalice of divinity. My life was changed from the business world to the ministry. When I am no longer on this plane, I believe that this divine entity, born that night on a lonely bench by the sea, will continue to use strangers and seemingly unrelated incidents to perpetuate its holy drama of the soul's awakening.

Arnold Michael

THE PREDICTION

As Anna met one of the vestal virgins in the corridor of the temple, she said, "Please inform the others that on this particular morning we will not have our class on the spoken records."

The vestal virgin was obviously disappointed. "But Princess Anna, you were to reveal how Moses told his people they could have wells they didn't dig and vineyards they didn't plant!"

Anna smiled at her impatient interest. "Tomorrow, child. Tomorrow, I will tell you."

At a door, Anna softly knocked. A mellow, deep voice invited her to enter. As she did, the gentle face of a huge priest lit up with joy. Rising from his table upon which an open scroll was opened, he stretched forth his hands and took hers in a greeting of warm affection and respect.

"Sit down and tell me why the high priestess visits a humble priest."

They sat facing each other.

"Halhul," Anna's voice was hardly more than a whisper. "I come for counsel and guidance from a dear friend."

"Usually, it is we who come to you for guidance and counsel." Halhul's tone was light, though he sensed the seriousness of her visit. For a moment, they just looked into each other's eyes where shone a mutual confidence and security of true friendship.

Anna spoke slowly and deliberately, choosing her words as though her very life depended upon their significance.

"Do you believe that the ways of God's love can take away one blessing with another blessing? My life in the temple, the thrilling wonder of being the keeper and teacher of the spoken records, records so holy that they cannot be entrusted to writing but are passed on from age to age by word of mouth. The wonder of this blessing is now threatened by another blessing."

Anna paused. A deep sigh trembled through her erect, slim body. For an instant, the poised wisdom usually radiating from her classical features was clouded with confusion, but only for an instant. Then she continued. "This new blessing is the wonder of the love of a very special man and the wonder of my love for him."

When she didn't say more, Halhul gently asked, "How does the wonder of one blessing deprive you of the wonder of another?"

Anna gazed out the window over the balustrade and down into the enclosed courtyards of the temple, then back to the eyes of her friend. Her voice was toneless as she answered. "I cannot marry him unless I leave the temple. Our laws demand that I marry a Jew and he is not a Jew."

Halhul's heart ached for his beloved Anna. Gently, he asked, "Do you want to tell me who he is? Do I know him?"

"Perhaps. He is frequently near the temple in the Gentiles' Court where he teaches his followers. That is where I saw him, listened to him, and knew I loved him. He saw me there. We talked many times. That's the way it happened."

She became silently absorbed in her feelings.

"But, who is he?" Halhul finally asked.

Anna looked into Halhul's eyes with a kind of pride and awe as she quietly explained. "A pious, wealthy prince of the family that ruled Palestine when the Persians were in control. He is the Hierophant in charge of the Persian School of the Magi located near my home in Nazareth. His name is Nakeeb Shah."

Halhul nodded his head excitedly. "I've seen him! He's magnificent. A fascinating speaker. I have mixed with his audience several times to hear the nature of his teaching. It is similar to ours: self-mastership toward godliness. It seems to me they have no special religion or dogma except seeking and living the truth. I did notice that they take much of their wisdom from the light of Zoroaster, which is natural since they are Persians."

Both were now silent with their thoughts and feelings.

Halhul was deeply thoughtful. Suddenly, he said, "Do I have your permission to speak with him as your friend?"

Anna was happily puzzled. She arose, as did Halhul. She took one of his huge hands in hers, looking up into his face with eyes glistening with gratitude. "You certainly do," she responded.

As Nakeeb Shah finished his talk to his followers in the Gentiles' Court, Halhul approached and spoke pleasantly to him. "I enjoyed and agreed with the substance of your message."

Nakeeb Shah smiled his appreciation and said cordially, "I have noticed you before in the group. May I know your name?"

"I am Halhul." He gestured to what he was wearing. "As you see, I am a priest from the temple."

Nakeeb Shah nodded pleasantly. "I am pleased to make your acquaintance and I appreciate your interest in our work."

He turned to leave. Halhul said, "May I speak with you as a close friend of Princess Anna?"

Nakeeb Shah's attitude was of patient, tolerant understanding as he nodded. He said, "We would have more privacy near the wall." He led the way toward the wall that enclosed the Gentiles' Court. When they reached it, he gazed with cordial tolerance into Halhul's face and waited.

Halhul began, "Because of the depth of our friendship, Anna told me of your wonderful love for each other. She is utterly distraught because our laws prohibit you from becoming man and wife. She knows I am talking with you, but not why. My purpose is to explore with you the possibility of making your marriage a reality."

Nakeeb Shah was instantly alert. "Is there a possibility?"

"The requirement would be that you become a Jew."

Nakeeb Shah's controlled excitement changed to controlled disappointment. Sadly, he murmured, "I know. But what would happen to my followers, all the people who depend on me for the truths by which they strive to live?"

Halhul's tone was rich with the authority of promise. "You could still lead them. You could still teach them the same truths."

"What do you mean?"

"I have listened to you enough to know there is no basic difference in our teachings. You teach there is but one God, the Father of us all, and so do we. You teach that our relationship to him is to love him with all our heart and mind and live by his truths, and so do we."

Nakeeb Shah nodded his head eagerly as Halhul spoke. Halhul paused and studied him with pleasure, then he said, "That takes care of the similarity of our relationship to God, which leaves only our human relationships. Are we also in agreement there?"

Nakeeb Shah became more thoughtful, then hopefully said, "Our attitude is taken from Zoroastrianism which states that nature only is good when it shall not do unto another whatever is not good for its own self."

Halhul laughed aloud with joy as he said, "Ours is almost verbatim. It is precisely this: What is hurtful to yourself, do not to another."

Nakeeb Shah's eyes were suddenly aglow with a new understanding. "Bless the unselfish wisdom of her love!" he murmured rapturously.

Halhul was puzzled. "I don't understand."

"Neither did I at the time. But now I do. When Anna and I would speak of the difficulty of our becoming man and wife, she would always point out her discovery of the similarities within the many different religions to which she has listened year after year here in the Gentiles' Court."

Nakeeb Shah chuckled with joy. "It always hurt me a bit, for I thought she was changing the subject, that there were things she felt were more important than our problem. But she wasn't changing the subject. She was trying to make me see the answer to our problem. She wanted the choice to become a Jew to be my idea. To come from me. Not from her!"

He looked deeply into Halhul's eyes, now aglow with

gladness for their happiness. "I am so grateful to you. Would you please send her to me so I can tell her that at long last I know what she has been trying to tell me. How soon can you set in motion the means by which my followers and I can become Jews?"

"It will be begun at once." Halhul turned to go.

Nakeeb Shah stopped him. "Wait! I have a question. Come with me for a moment."

He led Halhul out Court of the Gentiles gate. At the outer wall, he pointed to a rectangular-shaped strip of land. He said, "That strip of land next to the wall belongs to my family. My ancestors purchased it from the Hittites before David acquired his kingdom and the temple was built. Would it be permissible for me to build a wall on this strip in which my followers could live in comfort? Then tear down the intervening, uninhabitable wall so that my people would be living next to the Gentile's Court where we could gather for our talks and prayers?"

"The council would have to approve … but I'm certain they will."

Together they walked back into the court, both a reflection of joyous expectation. Nakeeb Shah suddenly stopped. "One more thing. Since you showed me the way for Anna and I to be together, would you perform the wedding ceremony?"

Halhul laughed happily, took Nakeeb Shah's shoulders in his hands and shook him with gentle affection to emphasize his answer. "It would be the most precious of all my performances."

When Nakeeb Shah was formally converted, he was given the Jewish name of *Joachim*. Halhul explained,

"This new name means 'the executive power of love, the pivotal center within man that preserves the unity and integrity of soul and body.'"

Nakeeb Shah replied, "I will cherish my name and strive to obey its guidance."

After the wedding ceremony, Anna and Joachim spent several happy days in his home and in hers so that the many servants in both homes would have the pleasure of serving the masters who were so esteemed and loved by them all. Then Anna returned to her work in the temple and Joachim supervised the construction of the living quarters being installed in the new wall of the Gentiles' Court.

Many happy years went by but because they had no children an anxiety began growing in their hearts that they might never have a child. According to the laws and traditions of the Jews, a childless marriage was condemned because it did not perpetuate God's Israel. Anna and Joachim kept their anxiety from each other, but individually prayed fervently for a child, vowing to dedicate it to God.

Some priests began reproaching Joachim when he brought his offerings to the altar. One said, "Your marriage to Princess Anna united the two oldest and noblest families in all Palestine, therefore a child from you would be the most wealthy and powerful in all Israel. Do you not feel the pressure of divine duty to provide us such a person?"

This condemnation caused Joachim to go into the wilderness to fast and pray in an effort to become worthy of a child. He did not tell Anna he was going because he could not think of a way without revealing what the priest had said. He was desperate, distraught, and confused.

When Joachim had been in the wilderness for some time, during his loneliness an angel of wonderful light suddenly stood beside him. Joachim was startled and afraid. The angel comforted him by saying, "Be not afraid, for I am an angel of the Lord sent by him that I might inform you that your prayers are heard. He hath heard you unjustly reproached for not having children and wants you to know that when he closes the womb of a woman, he does it so that he may open it again in a more wonderful manner, proving that that which is born is not of lust, but a gift of God for a special blessing to all.

"Was not Sarah, the first mother of the Hebrew nation, barren until her eightieth year and yet she brought forth Isaac through whom a blessing was made to the entire nation? And did not a similar thing happen to Rachel who brought forth Joseph, who was not only governor of Egypt, but he who delivered many nations from hunger?

"God has an even greater plan for your wife, for she shall bring you a daughter whom you shall call 'Mary.' According to your previous vow, she shall be dedicated to the Lord from her infancy. Mary shall, in a miraculous manner, be born of Anna who was barren. However, Mary, while yet a virgin, shall in an unparalleled way, bring forth a Son of the most High God who shall be called Jesus, and he shall be the savior of all nations.

"If your reason will not convince you that there have been significant conceptions in advanced years, I give you this sign of the truth of my word. When you return and arrive at the golden gate of Jerusalem, your wife will meet you there. She is very troubled that you have not returned and great will be her joy to see you."

Anna lay on the couch in her private quarters watching birds feeding their young in a nest outside her window. She was in deep despair both at the absence of Joachim and of her continual barrenness. She murmured to herself, "All God's creatures, even the birds, are joyously bringing forth their young. But not I. Oh, my poor Joachim! Would that I could comfort his unhappiness, wherever he is."

Suddenly, the angel appeared beside her. "Fear not, Anna. I am the angel who hath offered up your prayers before God and am now sent to inform you that a daughter will be born unto you who shall be called Mary, and who shall be *blessed above all women*. As a virgin maiden, not knowing any man, she shall bring forth a son in an unparalleled way, who by his grace, name, and works shall be the savior of the world.

"Arise, therefore, and go through Jerusalem and when you come to the golden gate, as a sign of this truth, you shall meet your husband for whose safety you have been so concerned. When you find this prophecy accomplished and see him there, then believe that all the other things I have told you shall likewise be accomplished."

According to the command of the angel, both Anna and Joachim started toward the place specified by the angel's prediction. Simultaneously, they approached the golden gate from opposite directions. Anna from within the city, Joachim from without. Simultaneously, also, they recognized each other and rushed into each other's arms. The gratitude and love they felt at seeing each other was multiplied by this proof of the angel's promise of a child.

With his cheek close to hers, Joachim whispered reverently, "The angel said that when God closes the womb of a woman, he does it so that he may, in a more wonderful manner, open it again as a special blessing to all life."

Anna trembled at his words. Both were overflowing with divine ecstasy. Anna put her forehead to his and, as she did, both thrilled from head to toe. With difficulty, Anna spoke. "I feel that at this instant I have conceived, conceived as a wondrous gift straight from the heart of God."

When nine months were fulfilled, Anna gave birth. She asked the midwife, "What have I brought forth?"

"It is a girl," the midwife answered.

In a joyful voice, Anna cried aloud. "The Lord hath this day magnified my soul!" And she laid the babe beside her.

When the days of her purification were accomplished, she nourished the babe at her breast and called her Mary.

When Mary was three years of age, she was formally dedicated to the temple. When Joachim relinquished her to the priest, the priest exclaimed, "Like David, she is a ruddy child, fresh from the sun, a child of God."

He held her up so that all could see, and as he did, Mary threw back her golden curls, turned her beautiful blue eyes to heaven, raised her baby hands aloft and sang a little song of praise and devotion of her own words and music.

The witnesses were silent in awe. The priest said, "As her ancestor David, she, too, will write poems and compose music. So I dedicate you, Mary, to be a candlestick of the House of David in the House of the Lord."

From that time on, Mary grew up in the temple. Many of her songs were sung in the temple choir in which she sang with her exceedingly sweet voice.

Joachim deeded all his property to Mary and appointed the priests her guardians in case of his death. Anna resumed her work in the temple. In gratitude to God, Joachim and Anna adopted a homeless child with the name Mary.

The friendship between Joachim and Halhul grew richer over the years and often Halhul spoke of Mary's unusual achievements in the temple. When Mary was thirteen, Joachim confided to Halhul the secret so holy that both Anna and he rarely referred to it, even to each other. Joachim hoped Halhul could provide him with a certain answer.

He said to Halhul, "When the angel told both Anna and me that our daughter would be the mother of the savior of all nations, he also said that she would conceive in an *unparalleled* way. What way could that be?"

Halhul was deeply moved. For a long moment, his only answer was a reverent silence. Joachim waited breathlessly for him to speak. A sigh of deep wonder shook Halhul's mighty frame. He looked up into Joachim's expectant eyes and murmured, "I do not know."

Joachim was obviously disappointed. "You were my only hope. I've waited a long time to ask you this question."

Halhul continued. "The word 'unparalleled' means nothing equal to it has ever happened before. We will just have to be content that something new is to happen in our world ... and happen soon! For Mary draws near the age, if she is to be the mother of the prophesied Messiah!"

Source material for "The Prediction" is from *The Lost Books of the Bible* by Rutherford Hayes Platt; a Meridan Book published by New American Library, Inc., 1301 Avenue of the Americas, New York, New York 10019; 1973, 1974.

CHAPTER 1

"You need not be frightened! Through your son shall humanity be awakened to the message I bring each night and morning in my symbolic death and resurrection!"

Again this strange prophecy was spoken into Mary's heart by the rising sun as it cleared the Mount of Olives. Anxiously, she looked behind her, searching the fronds of evergreens for the spying face of Zaele, a temple maiden of her own age. The evergreens concealed this isolated corner of the balustrade that ran around the Women's Court high in the temple. Not till yesterday had there ever been an intruder into Mary's little sanctuary.

All were supposed to be at their own private morning prayers, but yesterday morning Mary had detected the furtively inquiring eyes of Zaele peering through the evergreen. On being discovered, Zaele had fled, but Mary had been unable to remove the fear that Zaele might have overheard her talking to the sun.

Each morning, as long as Mary could remember, she had stood in this isolated corner of the balustrade and greeted the morning sun. The reason for these trysts with the rising sun was a wonderful secret buried deep within her young heart, a heart in which but recently had begun the murmurs of budding womanhood. And this particular morning the murmurs were more insistent than ever before.

1

Satisfied that Zaele had not dared again to leave her own prayers, Mary leaned against the familiar smoothness of the cool marble column and let her lingering gaze move out over the sanctuary gate of Nicanor, through the peristyle of Solomon's Porch, over the Garden of Gethsemane, across the Kidron Valley, and up the Mount of Olives. The sun had cleared the Mount and its reborn light brought new life to the waiting world. Pulsating circles of gold peeled from its circumference and moved toward her through the freshened ethers.

In tones low, clear, and sweet, she said, "Today I am fourteen. The time is here that I must leave the temple – and I am frightened!"

"You need not be alarmed," came the voice she had learned to love so long ago. The most authoritative voice she had heard, yet it held a gentleness so exquisite that she never failed to thrill with its sound. "That which is about to begin," it continued, "is but that for which we have been preparing since first you stood there, a lonely, bewildered child of three. You had been instructed that you must perform morning prayers in private, so each dawn you came, though you knew not what was expected of you."

The quality of gentleness increased and Mary's heart grew full as she remembered what the sun had meant to her through all her lonely years. "Each dawn you huddled against the cold base of your column and attempted to pray. You did not know how, so mostly you wept. Then you discovered that I too came every morning. I was something you could talk to, so you did. And many talks we have had. Tomorrow the priests will choose for you a husband, and your covenant with motherhood shall begin.

Be not frightened. You have prepared yourself well."

The voice ceased. As always when the voice had spoken, her fears were dispelled and confidence returned. Then behind her she heard a faint rustle among the evergreens. Turning quickly, she looked again into the suspicious eyes of her intruder of yesterday morning. Zaele had contributed more than any of the other maidens to Mary's loneliness and discomfort. Her dark beauty and vivacious temperament were more in accord with life outside the temple than within. Her parents had consecrated her to the temple as an infant, so until she was fourteen she would have to remain in the temple. She was constantly before the tribunal for rule infractions, so there was little doubt that when the time came she would go out into the world, provided she was chosen by a husband.

At every opportunity, she ridiculed Mary and the prophecies concerning her until all the loneliness and misery Mary had suffered in the temple were personified in this particular girl. A gleam of cunning flashed in Zaele's eyes, then she was gone.

Suddenly, Mary wanted desperately to be with her older cousin Elizabeth. Elizabeth was the wife of Zacharias. Zacharias was a high priest of the temple. During his turn to preside over temple ceremonies, Elizabeth was much in the temple. Although Zacharias was now at their home in Hebron, Elizabeth remained to be near Mary because of her upcoming betrothal.

In her private chamber, Elizabeth greeted Mary with her usual warmth and affection. Though Elizabeth's hair was gray, beneath it were bright, tranquil eyes and classic features. Her figure had remained firm, slender, and erect.

There had always been aspects of Mary's own life that she did not understand. Mary knew Elizabeth could explain these things if she would, for Elizabeth was a fount of understanding. But she was not indulgent. Her understanding did not always produce sympathy. More often, pure logic and justice were forthcoming, regardless of how difficult or unpleasant.

Though Mary loved Elizabeth with all her heart, she had confided but little in her for fear that that which she would have confided was weakness and self-pity. If it had been that, Elizabeth would not have hesitated to say so. Elizabeth was a mirror reflecting accurately the values of life uncolored by personal feelings.

"Beloved cousin," Mary said. "You are so wise. Tell me why so many of the maidens resent my presence here. It has been true as far back as I can remember. When I was seven, you told me that at the time I was consecrated to the temple, the high priest prophesied that I would be the mother of the promised Messiah. Surely, this would not generate their resentment, unless in their eyes I am unworthy of such honor."

Smiling with understanding at Mary's concern, Elizabeth motioned her to the bench beside her. "Precious child," she said, taking her hand. "In every woman's heart, young or old, within the temple and without, there is one great longing. Many of us succeed in keeping it concealed, but most of us at some time reveal it in our thoughts and deeds. It is our desire for a strong and noble husband."

Turning to Mary, she lifted a whimsical eyebrow and added, "If this strong and noble husband happens also to be rich, we try not to let it disturb us. The other maidens know that tomorrow the strongest, noblest, and wealthiest men in all Palestine will present themselves and, from those, a husband will be chosen for you."

Elizabeth patted Mary's hand and sighed. "Everyone knows more of these things than you do. In your heart, there is no room for them. Not only are you the prophesied mother of the Messiah, but you are also princess of the House of David and, as such, the wealthiest bride in all Judea.

"Are not the cities of Jerusalem and Bethlehem known as the Cities of David? To your family belongs all the lands, even the land upon which stands this temple. According to the laws of David, it cannot be sold. The buildings can be sold, but every year of Jubilee, the land reverts back to the House of David. Your wealth is boundless. That cannot be questioned.

"But it can be questioned whether or not you will be the mother of the Messiah because for six hundred years each princess of the House of David has hoped to be the one through whom the Messianic prophecy would be fulfilled."

Elizabeth paused, pensively shrugging her elegantly erect shoulders. "As yet, the promised messiah has not been born. The princesses of the House of David who were in position to bring him forth have failed. Hence, these have been considered imposters by the resentful, who, in their secret hearts, have felt that if Providence had permitted them to be born a princess of the House of David, they certainly could have given birth to the long-awaited Messiah."

Elizabeth patted Mary's hand lightly and continued with playful solemnity. "So, my child, until you show the world the Messiah, you, too, will be thought an imposter and as such, subject to the suspicious resentment of jealous hearts."

Mary's usually smooth forehead showed her perplexity. "Why, after all these years, did the high priest prophesy it would be me?"

"Perhaps because, like David, you were a ruddy child," Elizabeth answered. "A child fresh from the sun with blue eyes and light complexion, born into a land of dark hair, eyes, and skin."

Slowly, Mary turned on Elizabeth, eyes widened with a question. "The only one?"

Elizabeth nodded with gentle emphasis, then continued. "All these qualities place you apart from the others. They are awed, resentful, and jealous."

For a long time there was silence. Then with great effort, Mary spoke, her words coming slowly as though they had long been locked away. "I, too, am guilty of resentment," she began. "For years it has grown, little by little. There were nights when I cried myself to sleep with loneliness when all about me were those who could be called friends. Yet, day after day, I was avoided and seldom spoken to, until at times, I felt actually poisoned from the fumes of my own resentment."

"Blessed child," Elizabeth said tenderly. "Never has a young heart been more sorely tried and never have the trials been more valiantly overcome. Do not condemn yourself for your resentment. Were your heart less sensitive, less hungry for love, there would have been no resentment."

Elizabeth's words removed an aching burden from Mary. Never had she confided to anyone this great fear of her growing resentment. It had so profoundly shamed her that not even to her beloved cousin did she dare reveal its existence. Now that she had, she felt wonderfully relieved. But deep within her still was a question. Now that she had confessed the existence of her resentment, would she be able to tear it completely out of her heart?

There was another thing that disturbed her. She had never been able to share with Elizabeth her secret communications with the sun. It wasn't that she feared Elizabeth's disapproval or lack of understanding; it was more a loyalty to that which the sun meant to her. That which the sun represented was beyond discussion with human beings, even with Elizabeth.

Mary remembered the many, many times her only companion had been the sun, although she had hungered to be included in the whispered secrets so avidly indulged in by the pairs and groups of other maidens. Also, she had wondered why her mother, the Priestess Anna, though much in the temple, spent no more time with her than with anyone else. Often she had wanted to ask Elizabeth about this, but felt in some way it would be improper. Since she was leaving the temple tomorrow and did not know when she would see Elizabeth again, she overcame her former reluctance.

"There is much I do not understand about my mother. I would remove from my heart this misunderstanding before I go from the temple to begin my other life. If it is wrong that these questions live in my heart, forgive me, but please do not deny me their answers."

Affectionate understanding kindled in Elizabeth's eyes. "Ask them, my child. I will do my best with their answers."

"During the years I have been here," Mary began with difficulty, "my mother has been no nearer to me than to the other maids. She seemed always to have so much to do. Seldom has a week passed that I have not seen her, yet her attitude toward me has never changed."

Mary placed her hand over her heart. "Something here," she murmured, "longs for my mother's affection. Should I not have that feeling?"

Mary was surprised to see Elizabeth's eyes grow moist. However, when she spoke, there were no tears in her voice. Her tone was impersonal, a trifle harsh, as though she were chiding Mary for harboring such critical thoughts of her mother's attitude. "When you were three," Elizabeth stated, "your mother consecrated you to the temple, thus relinquishing all claim to you. Henceforth, your development was to be the temple's responsibility. Thus, your mother could contact you only in the capacity of the temple priestess that she is.

"Your mother is a wonderful woman. That which has been denied you was denied her also. The hunger within your mother's heart for you is just as great, if not greater, than your own for her. Your mother holds a position in the temple never before held by a woman. To her is entrusted the teaching of the Spoken Records. These records are not written, but given from age to age by word of mouth. In this way, not only are the records perpetuated, their secret mysteries protected from the profane.

"These mysteries are those which were given to Moses on the Mount that he, in turn, gave to Joshua and the chosen forty. It is your mother's responsibility to teach these mysteries to the priests and vestal virgins and she is the authority to whom all refer disputes." Elizabeth's voice softened. "So you see, just as in your life, for the sake of the many, much has been denied you. Her life, too, has been dedicated, dedicated to the perpetuation of truth as humankind knows it."

Mary was weeping silently. "My beautiful, wonderful mother!" she whispered. "Why did I not ask these questions long ago? Then I would have understood. When the yearnings came, I would know she felt them, also. I could have turned my yearnings into a shield to protect us both from the hurt of that which was denied us."

Elizabeth placed a comforting hand on Mary's shoulder, then suddenly rose to her feet, quickened with a thought. "My child, you came from the union of the two oldest and noblest families in Palestine. That union brought into harmony the two most powerful religions in the world. None of these things happen by chance. The lives of your mother and father and the lives of their mothers and fathers for generations were lived according to a plan. Its fulfillment shall be in your son. The fulfillment begins tomorrow when your husband will be selected."

The tremendous responsibility that was hers suddenly swept over Mary, leaving her weak and frightened. Such strong and illustrious forebears! Such selflessness! Magnificence of purpose! She felt no different from anyone else. No special strength was hers to carry through and fulfill this plan begun so long ago. If such strength existed, she did not feel it.

She was grateful when a knock came on Elizabeth's chamber door, for she feared Elizabeth would soon discover her fright and possibly interpret it as weakness.

When Elizabeth returned from answering the door, Mary was startled by her pallor. Her face was as pale as parchment and her usually bright eyes were dulled and flecked with red. Her voice was dry and cramped with distress. "Mary," she said, ever so gently. "A special tribunal meeting has been called and they have sent for you!"

Mary's heart seemed to be in her throat. The tribunal usually met but once each month to pass judgment and punishment on those guilty of transgressing the laws of the temple. Only some grave infraction would cause the convening of a special session. "What could it mean?" Mary whispered aloud to herself.

With an effort, Elizabeth spoke. "The vestal virgin who was sent for you told me that it had something to do with you being guilty of sun worshipping."

A cold hand tightened on Mary's throat. Now she knew the reason for the unexplained fear caused by Zaele's eyes as she peered at her through the evergreens this morning. So shocked was Mary that she could not raise her head.

Tilting Mary's chin, Elizabeth gazed lovingly into her eyes and asked, "Is there anything you would like to tell me? Perhaps, I could help. Otherwise, you must go at once for the messenger waits to take you to the court."

Mary could only shake her head. Desperately, she wanted to explain to Elizabeth what had happened, but to tell anything at all, she would have to describe her morning communions with the sun from the beginning. However, it would be impossible now in a few words to justify herself, especially with the treat of an impending trial before the temple tribunal. To speak under such circumstances, she felt would be disloyal to the sun.

"Not now, beloved cousin," she managed to say. Then, summoning all her strength, she strode from Elizabeth's chamber and out to the vestal virgin waiting to escort her to the court.

Mary had never been brought before the temple's tribunal and its solemn austerity struck new fear to her already fluttering heart. On a tier of marble benches sat twelve priests, the purple robes of their office accentuating the somber severity of their faces.

To one side of the huge, cavernous courtroom sat Zaele, obviously pleased with herself. On the opposite side, Mary was seated. A short, rotund priest with beady black eyes and small hands that he constantly rubbed together, arose from his seat on the bench and bade Zaele to come to the center of the court.

Mary recognized him as Ananias. She was not surprised that he was conducting the investigation. From bits of gossip she had overheard, she realized that it was generally known that he was happiest when functioning in this capacity. Also, she had heard how he had effected a division among the priesthood. Many of the younger priests were under his influence and opposed to venerable Halhul, the chief of the Sanhedrin, who maintained a generous attitude toward the people in the temple. Halhul's presence among the twelve priests enabled Mary's breath to come more easily.

With a defiant glance at Mary, Zaele marched to the center of the room where a black circle was inlaid in the white marble floor. Ananias instructed Zaele. "Repeat to the tribunal that which you told me concerning Mary's activities when she should have been at her private morning prayers."

With another gloating glance at Mary, Zaele turned to the tier of priests. "As I was returning from my private prayers this morning, I heard a voice coming from a secluded place on the east balustrade. I parted the evergreens and saw Mary. She was not upon her knees, but standing with her back against a column and gazing directly into the sun." Zaele paused while she drew herself higher. Tilting her head for emphasis, she slowly and deliberately stated the words she knew would be most condemning. "And while she looked into the sun, I heard her voice. She was talking to the sun! I could not heart the words, but I could hear her voice."

Ananias motioned her to her seat and called Mary into the black circle. "Are you a sun worshipper?" he demanded.

Mary lifted her eyes and gazed passively toward him, but she did not speak.

"Answer me, child!" Ananias snapped impatiently, his small eyes beginning to burn. "Have you been using our holy temple as an altar for Shamash, the forbidden sun god?"

Mary continued to stare at her accuser without answering.

Angrily, Ananias turned to the other priests. "Her guilt is obvious, else she would deny it! Imagine our ridicule among the people and the Romans when it is learned that the prophesied mother of the messiah is a worshipper of Shamash, the sun god."

Producing a scroll from within the bulges of his robe, he said, "I will read you the law of Moses concerning such practice: 'Take heed therefore unto yourselves, lest you corrupt yourselves and make a graven image and lest you lift up your eyes to heaven and see the sun, moon, stars, and host of heaven, and should be driven to worship them and to serve them which the Lord God has divided and given unto all nations beneath the heavens.'"

Replacing the scroll, Ananias spoke again to the court. "It is my opinion that the conduct of this maiden demands that we take steps to protect the honor of our prophets. We have been in error. The promised Messiah could not come from one so unworthy, one who defiles our temple and defiles our laws. We can let it be known that she has rededicated herself to the temple and will not take a husband, that the mother of the Messiah is yet to appear."

There was an animated stir of approval among most of the priests. Mary felt like a witness to a scene in which she had no part. She was numb, dazed beyond the point of further reaction. The stir increased as the priests argued among themselves. Then it ceased abruptly as majestic old Halhul came to his feet, demanding silence.

"Ananias," he said, in a clear, resonant voice that held a twinge of accusation. "If the child were guilty of all you charge, her guilt would not be so grave. Suppose she did talk to the sun? What harm is there in that? We all know the ancient law of Moses. In his day, such a law was needed for our people were wont to worship anything beyond their comprehension, and all heavenly bodies were beyond their comprehension. It was Moses' task to awaken his people to the truth of the one God, Jehovah. And for an age, we have worshipped none but Jehovah."

The accusing tone in Halhul's voice increased. "Today, because you fear this little sunflower, you attempt to fasten importance to a conflict of thought which lost its significance a thousand years ago! Even if it was a crime to talk to the sun, she has not admitted doing so. Youth is fraught with a fertile imagination. Whether she talked to the sun or imagined she did is of little consequence."

Pausing, Halhul gazed gently down at Mary's pitiful little figure standing in the center of the immense courtroom
with its vaulted and expansive ceilings and columns. "Poor
child," he continued. "There has been no one else to
whom she could talk. Everyone has been afraid that an
overture of friendship would be interpreted by others as an
attempt to identify themselves with the royal House of
David. It is surprising that something more serious than
talking to the sun has not resulted from so abnormal a
life."

Halhul's gentle tones ceased. His voice held the promise of unpleasant justice as he turned his attention to Zaele.
"Your intentions are very obvious," he accused. "At the
next tribunal meeting, you are scheduled to answer for
several infractions. You thought this would influence our
clemency!"

Halhul lowered his voice in a confidential note.
"Ananias," he said. "Your part is not quite so obvious, yet
it can be recognized. For some time, you and your young
followers have attempted to increase the gold in our coffers through diverse channels. Do you think I know not of
your traffic with the Romans?

"My followers and I are getting old. The time will soon
come when we will be no more. Then you and your followers can do as you please with the temple and the people who worship here. That is, unless someone so powerful with the people that you and your avarice could not
stand against him should come forth and confront you."

Halhul's voice became lower and more accusing.
"Could it be, Ananias, that you are afraid the promised

messiah, prophesied to be born of this maiden, might be the one to spoil your dreams of greed? And by discrediting Mary now, you wish to prevent the coming of this Messiah?" Halhul's voice cracked out as a whip. "In my opinion, the only guilt is upon the head of the accusers!"

This time there was no stirring among the priests. Ananias' face was a pale green. Surreptitiously, he glanced at his followers for support. They were too frightened by Halhul's words to return his glance. With as much grace as he could muster, Ananias arose and dismissed the tribunal.

Mary hardly realized it was over until the vestal virgin who had come for her had put her to bed in her little room and, having arranged her covers as comfortably as possible, departed.

A moment later, she was aware of others in her room and their strong waves of protective love. Forcing her eyes open, she saw Elizabeth standing at one side of her bed. On the other side, stood her mother, who, as always, stood magnificently poised. As Anna looked down at Mary, the impersonal expression faded from her lovely face. Dropping to her knees, she gathered Mary into her arms and holding her daughter's head against her breasts, she murmured over and over, "My baby, my baby!"

Mary thrilled with an indescribable sweetness. She had never felt less like weeping, yet from her lips came soft whimpering sounds. The communicative sounds of a babe talking to its mother. In her case, repressed sounds, finally finding their utterance and bringing forth exquisite relief and a new maturity.

CHAPTER 2

L ong before the sun was due the next morning, Mary
stood against the cool smoothness of her column,
waiting. The sweetness of her mother's protective presence, as it had wafted her exhausted body into blissful
sleep, still lingered.

Awakening in the early morning hours, she had found
her mother gone. Mary would have believed it all a dream
had not the effects of her mother's presence been so undeniable.

However, this new found joy was overshadowed by
memories of the tribunal scene. Through her the sun had
been placed on trial, publicly defiled by such people as
Ananias and Zaele. Her flesh cringed with revulsion as she
remembered the details. The main issue had been whether
or not she was worthy to be the mother of the Messiah as
had been prophesied of her.

In her heart of hearts, she had hoped that if the Messiah
were born of her, it would be the result of a natural course
of events and that nothing special would be demanded of
her. She did not feel that she possessed any special qualifi-
cations. But now, she was beginning to believe that much
depended upon her for which she was inadequate, and she
was sorely afraid.

Many times before, she had stood as she now stood,
her slim, folded arms hugging a thumping heart, waiting
for the sun and the assurance it brought. She remembered

that previous problems were always dissolved by the time the rays of the sun reached the Garden of Gethsemane.

The mountainside sloping down to the valley of Kidron, just opposite the city's walls, always remained wrapped in sleeping shadows until the sun cleared its peak. Then its rays crept down the gentle slopes, patiently and thoroughly arousing to the new day every vale by tenderly removing their velvety covers of the night.

Nestled in the foothills and clearly visible from Mary's sanctuary was the Garden of Gethsemane. She could watch the light of the morning sun reach down and lift its shadows, bathing in fresh golden light its olive trees standing among blossoming flowers – pansies, stocks, pinks, anemones, or rose of Sharon – according to their season. When the light reached the garden, in spite of how strong had been her doubts generated during the night before, her apprehensions were lifted. The Garden of Gethsemane, reborn under the light of a new day, became a never-failing shield against the thrusts of her own misgivings.

Shivering from the cold preceding the dawn, Mary wondered when the garden was reborn today if her fears would again be replaced by confidence. The eastern heavens began to turn from black to gray, and from gray to varying shades of purple. The sky soon became light blue as a host of orange tints heralding the approach of the sun fanned across the sky. In the center of the flaming rays appeared the first golden crown of the rising sun. As it began its climb over the Mount of Olives, Mary spoke. "Much has happened since yesterday," she began with contrite humility. "I was discovered talking to you. We were placed on trial. They tried to make something unholy of us."

Removing her gaze from the sun, she bowed her head.
That which she now wanted to say was dear to her heart.
"There is nothing more holy to me than you and the words
you speak to me. Because of the trial, I feel that through
me, you have been blemished. Perhaps Ananias is right
and I am unworthy to be the Messiah's mother. Today I
am to be betrothed that my motherhood can begin. But
today, more than any other day, I feel inadequate."

Immediately the gentle authority of the beloved voice
vibrated in her anxious heart. "For fourteen years, since
the day of your birth, have I waited for this day, the day
when you should have proved your fidelity to me.
Yesterday, you were willing to suffer whatever punishment
was forthcoming rather than utter my name in the courtroom. Your faithfulness has proven that you are capable of
helping me in the work that is mine.

"This work is to demonstrate to humankind that the
death so feared does not exist. Each day I shine upon the
earth. Each morning I come fresh and bright and sing my
way across the sky. But people see me not. Their eyes are
fastened upon their feet and hands, things they can touch,
leaving their hearts cold and empty."

Mary braced herself against the smooth coolness of the
marble column for strength and contact with her own
world. Never before had anyone overcome death. Her
senses swam. Frantically, she strove to understand the
meaning of these strange, wondrous words.

As though reading her feelings, the sun continued.
"Listen closely to the story I tell. Parts of it you will
understand now. Other parts, not until later.

"At the beginning of time, the planet earth was dark. A
great being living in the sun offered to take abode on the

darkened earth in order to assist in earth's progress toward light. This being is *Love*. He is already known by many names to countless races, but always the theme of his song is the same.

"When the hearts of earth grow cold and lonely, the darkness increases. This darkness is reflected to us from the moon, just as our light is reflected to you from the moon. It is again time for this being to descend and nourish the hungry hearts of earth by dispelling darkness with light. However, only through those who live on earth, can earth be made more light. So, if this being is to bring light, he must do so as life on earth. He must become a man!

"There is a great difference between the rhythms of the sun and the rhythms of the earth. In order for this being to come to earth, his rhythm must be so altered that he can be born of woman and wear the earthly garb of flesh. But only so slow can his rhythm become. In order for him to reach the earth, the woman through whom he is to arrive must increase her vibration to a rate that harmonizes with his slowed rhythm.

"Love descends from sun to earth! But earth must reach forth a welcoming hand, else love can reach it not. You Mary, can be this welcoming hand. The purity of your heart is bright with a light that we upon the sun can see. Light and rhythm are the same. Your rhythm reaches high. You can give birth to this being of love! In flesh of your flesh can the light of the sun walk upon the earth as a man to awaken humanity's awareness of its own true nature and to reveal to all the truth of their Godhood!

"Your son will be able to demonstrate that love is the only power by which humanity holds dominion over both life and death. This Messiah, spoken of by the prophets,

shall mean more to the world than the prophets dreamed.
He will be misunderstood by his generation, and by many
generations to come, because people are not ready for
what the Messiah will bring.

"But his coming will quicken humanity's preparedness
and the age will come when the Messiah will be understood. At that time, little mother, will my commission be
achieved."

Mary was afire. Such glorious tidings! The fact that a
man was to overcome death so completely consumed her
heart and mind that for some time the realization that she
was capable of being his mother did not penetrate her consciousness.

"*Little mother* the sun called me," she repeated over and
over to herself. Her entire being still vibrated from the thrill
of hearing that wondrous voice call her *little mother*. Then,
all at once, its tremendous portent swept over her. She could
hardly breathe. Not only was the messiah to be King of the
Jews, but he was to demonstrate humankind's dominion
over death. And she could be the mother of this man.

All of this was more than she could sustain alone. She
must see Elizabeth at once. Elizabeth's strength, wisdom,
and love would support her and give her courage. So anxious was she to see Elizabeth that she could not walk; she
must run. To escape comment on her haste, she must avoid
the more frequently used halls and walks. Next to the
balustrade was a seldom-used walk, mostly hidden by
shrubs and evergreens. Lifting the folds of her skirts in
one hand and clasping her veil with the other, she sped
along this concealed path.

Rounding a curve, Mary came to an abrupt stop. Seated
at a pool in the center of the walk was Zaele. Her head and

shoulders were bare and artistically arranged in her dark, luxuriant hair was a cluster of bright red flowers. She had obviously been admiring herself in the pool. The removal of her veil, her bare shoulders, and the flower ornaments in her hair were unforgivable infractions of temple laws, especially at a time when she should have been at her private morning prayers.

Zaele was startled and frightened, but as she recognized Mary, her fear changed to anger. Snatching the flowers from her hair, she crushed them in her hand and then threw them into the pool. Tossing her hair in defiance, she snapped accusingly, "Following me so you can report me to old Halhul!" Then a resentful rage consumed her. "Only you can have any man in Palestine for a husband. I have no rich dowry." Her voice developed a sarcastic rasp as she continued. "Neither am I to be the mother of the Messiah. You ... you sun worshiper!"

To Mary, this last taunt was blasphemous. The resentment, gathering since first she realized that she was different from the other maidens, rushed unchecked into her heart, bursting into unbridled resentment. Resentment that her life had been ridiculed before the tribunal yesterday, resentment at this girl in whom all resentment was personified, this girl who dared profane her sun and the altar of her life.

The sudden, unexpected fury in Mary's face frightened Zaele to her feet. Taking a step toward her, Mary raised her hand to strike this personification of the cause of her years of misery. So frightened was Zaele that she could not move. For an instant, Mary's hand remained poised. In that instant, Zaele sufficiently overcame her fright to turn and flee.

Mary remained rigid, her hand still raised to strike Zaele. Gradually, her mind cooled. Her body relaxed. Bewildered, she stared at her trembling uplifted hand. Slowly, she lowered it as though it were contemptible and did not belong to her. Her entire body twitched violently as though it had been cruelly lashed.

The fumes of resentment evaporated and reason returned. Mary realized the fear she had harbored all along was true. She *was* unworthy! That which she had fought and conquered, all these years in the temple, had overcome her on the last day, the day she was to have left her temptation forever. One capable of the emotion she had just experienced could not bring the Messiah into the world – especially the one of whom the sun just spoke.

Holding as far from her as possible the still trembling hand, she stared at it with wide-eyed incredulity. Her attention focused upon its vibratory motion. The words of the sun concerning vibration and rhythm were frightfully fresh in her mind. Gladly would she have severed from her body this member, trembling yet from the poison of resentment. She was sufficiently familiar with the meaning of vibration to know that her trembling hand was a manifestation of a vibration, but vibration in its lowest form, caused by the emotion of resentment. A hand trembling from desire to strike another could never attain the exquisite rhythm of which the sun spoke, could never be the instrument of love's descension upon earth!

With anguished effort, she forced herself to continue toward Elizabeth's chamber. She would confess and Elizabeth could tell the priests. Then it would be announced there would be no betrothal. As Ananias had accused, the mother of the Messiah was yet to be born to the House of David.

Mary finally reached the curtain leading to Elizabeth's chamber. There her strength failed utterly. To part the curtain and enter was impossible. Her lowered glance fastened upon the hand that had lifted itself so readily under the impulse of resentment. It now hung as if lifeless.

Suddenly, a new strength moved through Mary, born of a condemnation of this member so willing to offend her a moment ago and now hiding behind an inability to open the way to confession of its deed. With this new strength of condemnation, Mary forced the hand to part the curtain. In the deliberate slowness of her movement, she felt a vague sense of justice. The hand was being forced to consciously provide its own punishment.

Elizabeth sat on a marble bench. The sweetness of her familiarity was accentuated because Mary's hopes associated with it were gone. Elizabeth's stiff embroidered cap beneath her flowing veil mocked Mary because it was the headdress all married women wore. Many times, Mary had pictured herself crowned with the warm dignity of such a cap, but the possibility seemed gone now forever.

Elizabeth greeted her with a smile so sincere and radiant that deep inside something gave way. Suddenly, Mary was a tired, bewildered little girl wanting only love and sympathy. Running across the chamber, she threw herself upon her knees, burying her head in Elizabeth's lap. Quietly and desperately, she sobbed.

With wordless patience, Elizabeth stroked her head. When the violent sobbing had lessened, Elizabeth spoke. "Such painful grief must surely come from a self-inflicted wound. Tell me why you weep, my child. Perhaps my more seasoned heart can absorb a portion of the pain."

Without lifting her head from the security of
Elizabeth's lap, Mary poured forth the story of her unworthiness. She told how Zaele's words had provoked such
great resentment within her heart that violence of hand
could easily have been the result. She confessed that with
such capabilities of evil lying dormant within her, she
could not be she of whom the prophets spoke.

Elizabeth's answer was to take the hand that clasped
her knee so frantically and press its feverish palm to the
cool firmness of her own. Not until the tension of Mary's
hand lessened did Elizabeth speak. "My child, it is true we
must not be slave of our emotions. But neither should we
be void of spirit. What to you is an unforgivable sin, to
another might not merit remembering until the next hour.
If the cloth were not so white, undetectable would be the
spot. Fear not for your unworthiness. Worthiness has no
better proof than confession of its lack."

Turning her head, Mary stared anxiously and hopefully
into the face of her friend. So much did she love this face
and so sensitive was she to its moods that even now, miserable as she was with her own problems, she was aware
of a new and different something in Elizabeth's face. Its
beauty was the same. But always before there had been a
vague loneliness that now was gone. In its place was a
subtle, undefinable joy.

Elizabeth returned Mary's inquiring gaze with an
encouraging smile, but as she spoke her voice was firm
with purpose. "You have a destiny to fulfill. Doubt and
pain are markers of your progress in its fulfillment.
Emotions must be overcome. To be overcome, they must
be exposed. The exposure is painful, their subjugation
always uncertain."

With protective affection, Elizabeth pressed Mary's face close to her lap. Her eyes were pensively distant as she continued. Mary recognized the tone of prophecy in her voice. "Your life is to be very unusual, my child. Through you the stigma of womanhood shall disappear from the earth. No longer will woman be chattel and slave. Motherhood will cast aside her contemptible rags, wearing in their place royal silks.

"And, through you, man will grow toward his maturity. In every man is the seed of good. This seed will grow only in the soil of love. Also, in every man is love of mother that he hides from the scorn of other men."

Mary was accustomed to Elizabeth's profound prophecies. But never before had the words stirred tiny golden bells deep within her. The prophetic tone increased. "Because of you, man will admit his love of mother as proudly as he now flaunts his shield of war. In this, his first professed love, man's dormant seed of good will begin its growth. The growth of good in the ages to come will extend outward. From mother to brother it will spread. And the time will be when the good in man will dominate his will toward all, even to the stranger in foreign lands. All women will be his mother! All men, his brothers!"

The meaning of Elizabeth's words was not clear to Mary. She could not understand how the result of her life could bring about such wonderful changes in the present attitude of man. However, it was clear that Elizabeth did not feel her unbridled passion had rendered her unfit to carry on. She could still be betrothed and leave the temple.

Elizabeth's fondness for her would not have affected her opinion. Elizabeth was always just. Mary searched her heart for any withheld evidence. She found none. True, she had not mentioned the sun, but the sun had naught to do with her resentment.

Thinking of the sun, Mary realized the words of Elizabeth and those of the sun were similar. Both had spoken of a love whose power it was to awaken the good in humanity. Suddenly, Mary was more confident than ever. The sun and Elizabeth, her two sources of strength, had told her the same things concerning the wondrously incredible, incomprehensible things that she was capable of doing and becoming. She would try not to doubt their wisdom, but pray that if they were right, the ability to fulfill their prophecies would be hers when needed.

Elizabeth was speaking again, this time in a joyous, confidential whisper. "In order that you may have evidence of this truth I speak and see the pattern of purpose already begun in our lives, I will share with you a wondrous secret.

"The day of our betrothal, Zacharias and I dedicated ourselves to the will of God in the hope that He would bless us with a son. But the years of our fruitfulness went by, leaving barren our marriage." Elizabeth paused and gazed steadily into Mary's eyes. "Long have I passed the age of conception. Yet, at this very moment, I am with child! A holy child! Our prayers are being answered in greater measure than we could dream."

Never before had Mary seen a face more beautiful as Elizabeth continued. "Long after we had despaired of its arrival, it comes. Not just a child, any child, as we had prayed, but a holy one."

Mary leaped to her feet to be beside Elizabeth. With happy impatience she awaited the remainder of the story, her own problems utterly forgotten. Now she understood the quiet joy in her cousin's face where before had been resigned loneliness. Mary thrilled to her toes at such a miraculous happening. After all these years Elizabeth was with child.

"How wonderful!" she murmured, hoping breathlessly that Elizabeth would see fit to tell her more. Elizabeth's manner sobered. "Zacharias hoped to be the priest who would choose your husband tomorrow, but alas he has lost his power of speech and is now in Hebron."

Mary had heard whisperings concerning the departure of Zacharias, but their insinuations were so variant she had heeded none of them. Elizabeth explained. "Zacharias was burning incense before leading the prayers of the multitudes awaiting him in the court. Suddenly, on the right side of the incense altar, an angel of the Lord appeared. Zacharias was stunned and fearful."

"The angel spoke. 'Fear not, Zacharias, for your prayers have been heard. Elizabeth, your wife, shall bear you a son and you shall call his name John. In the sight of the Lord, he shall be great. He shall drink no wine and from his mother's womb be filled with Holy Breath. In the spirit of Elias, he shall go before the coming of the Lord and turn many of the children of Israel to their God.'"

Such happenings so awed Mary she felt faint and her heart pounded wildly.

Elizabeth continued. "Recovering from his fear, Zacharias said to the angel, 'This cannot be for I am an old man and my wife well stricken in years.'

"Then the angel said to Zacharias, 'I am Gabriel. I stand in the presence of God and am sent to bring you these glad tidings. Because you believe not my words, you shall be dumb, unable to speak, until these things I tell you have been performed in their season.'

"The people waiting in the court were restless, wondering that Zacharias tarried so long in the temple. And much did they marvel when he did appear, unable to speak to them."

A sense of pity for Zacharias penetrated Mary's spellbound consciousness. "Poor Zacharias!" she exclaimed.

Elizabeth nodded her head in pensive agreement. "Yes," she said slowly. "Zacharias, the man, and Zacharias, the priest, have not been very harmonious companions. As a man, he has done many things of which the priest did not approve. And, at times, the opinion of the man so confounded the priest that the priest knew not what he believed. Thus, when the angel told Zacharias, the priest, he was to have a son; Zacharias, the man, remembering his years, raised his voice in disbelief. So his voice was taken from him."

Elizabeth paused, smiling slightly, a deep light of affectionate understanding for her husband shining in her eyes. "Now that both the man and the priest have time to think, I imagine both have concluded that in the miracle of God there is no difference between suddenly being struck dumb and one's wife conceiving after the passing of his season of potency."

Glancing at Mary's intent, doleful face, Elizabeth clasped her shoulders and playfully shook them. "Come, my child, let's not waste any more sympathy on Zacharias. He can still write what he wishes. And, believe me, he was never more content. One would think for forty years I had plied him constantly with idle chatter and stupid questions, so pleased is he now with his inability to answer me. He just walks in his garden and follows me with his eyes – eyes that still seem to doubt what they see, but nevertheless eyes that are extremely pleased with themselves and with that which goes on around them."

Laughing softly, Elizabeth kissed Mary's brow and arose to depart. Turning back, she said, "Your mother and father await with the others in the court. Your father has brought a friend of his. Perhaps, you remember him. Joseph, of the Carpenter Tribe?"

Mary shook her head. "Father has spoken of him," she replied. "He seems to very much admire this Joseph."

"Everyone does," Elizabeth said quietly. "He is a wonderful man, a descendant of David through the House of Nathan who trained his sons to be designers of synagogues. They are called the Carpenter Tribe. Joseph inherited all the lands of the Carpenter Tribe. A wise and wealthy man!"

After Elizabeth had gone, Mary wondered why she had suddenly spoken of this Joseph with such feeling. However, the wonders of the forthcoming events quickly excluded all irrelevant thoughts. But just as though it were not irrelevant, the name of Joseph of the Carpenter Tribe and the way Elizabeth had spoken of him recurred to her mind as she thought of the prospective husbands gathering around the altar in the court.

But her young heart had many things to ponder regarding that which was about to take place in that part of the temple, and she hurried away to make herself ready.

CHAPTER 3

The muffled sound of many sandal-clad feet approaching outside her chamber door announced to Mary the arrival of the temple women who were to form the procession in which she would descend to the court where Priest Halhul was to choose her husband. Mary's heart quickened. The beginning of her new life was at hand. It would be a completely strange life, and, if an unsuitable husband were chosen, a very fearful life.

Glancing about the austere room in which she had lived and remembering how unhappy most of the years had been, she felt a momentary surge of strength and impatience to greet the strange, to welcome the new. On the crest of this urge, she parted her curtained door and took her place in the waiting procession.

Leading the procession was her mother, High Priestess Anna. Behind her were the priestesses and vestal virgins, then came the temple maidens. Mary's place was at the head of the maidens.

It all seemed unreal to her. The women in the procession were like strangers instead of people she had lived with for years. She even imagined she saw open resentment in some of the faces. A quick glance at Zaele, near the rear, left no doubt. Zaele walked with obvious awareness of her own personal charm and equal disdain for the purpose of the procession.

Down into the court they moved with solemn dignity.

From the window of her room, Mary had often looked out
upon Roman soldiers marching through the streets with a
prisoner in their midst. She wondered why she should
think of such things at this time. Maybe because the prisoner, like herself, was always in the middle of the procession. Did she feel she was a prisoner? A prisoner of
prophecy? Her life bound and predetermined by the hopes
and fears of others?

For a fleeting instant, she allowed herself this self-
indulgent sense of sacrifice, but only for an instant. Then,
remembering her covenant with the sun and the glorious
secret mysteries Elizabeth and she shared, she proudly
stepped forward toward this adventurous life that was
ahead of her.

On a little balcony beneath the altar, the women seated
themselves in the order of their arrival. Mary stood alone
before the altar, the same altar upon which were sacrificed
lambs and doves for the remission of the sins of those who
paid for the ceremony. Extending from the level of the
altar was a latticed porch leading into the Holy Place.
Often Mary stood among the people at the salutation hour
and watched as various priests, in turn, led the temple
services, but never before had she been so impressed with
the solemn grandeur of the Marble Court of the priests.

Never before had Halhul's priestly garb so affected her.
Erect and motionless, he stood beside the high altar.
Gathered below were many men. When first Mary looked
out on them, she was conscious only of forms and colors.
Their striped cloaks of reds, yellows, blacks, and blues
with girdles of impressive silk signified to all the measure
of their wealth. Halhul had announced, days ago, that all
who wished to be among those chosen from must bring

with them a shepherd's staff. Mary had never seen so
many men and all seemed to have a shepherd's staff at
their side.

In the space reserved for her kin, Mary saw her mother
and father, both resplendent in their pride and dress.
Beside her mother stood Elizabeth, and Mary's heart
warmed to her smile of sweet assurance.

In Elizabeth's posture, Mary sensed a new dignity. As
daughter of Aaron and as a temple teacher, Elizabeth had
always carried her height and classical features with
queenly grace. But now, there was something new. Mary
thrilled with realization that this new dignity must come
from their secret – the life developing within Elizabeth
would add dignity to any woman's bearing. It added dignity to the entire estate of man.

Mary tried to imagine how it must feel to carry within
one's womb a holy child. But try as she might, such poten-
tial ecstasy was beyond her imagination. She could generate no feeling comparable to the subtle quality of joy she
sensed in Elizabeth. Elizabeth had told her that after today
she would retire to her home in Hebron to take away her
reproachful presence from among the men because to
them, the gray of her hair rebuked the growth in her
womb.

A sudden hush spread throughout the court. Everyone
lifted his eyes to Halhul who had moved from his statue-
like stillness and raised his arms and face heavenward.
Abruptly, he lowered them, and seven members of the
priesthood came from seven antechambers of the court.
Moving among the crowd, they began gathering from the
men the shepherd's staffs that indicated they were among
those from whom Halhul was to choose.

As the crowd stilled a bit, Mary caught her first glimpse of the man standing beside her father. In contrast to the clashing colors and shuffling feet of the others, this man wore a pure white robe and stood with the simple majesty of a cedar upon the slopes of Lebanon. There was a virility in his slender, erect stance that held fast her gaze. The rays of the noonday sun danced with lightning toes in the silvery abundance of his curled hair. His skin was olive, but so clear it seemed to glow.

This must be Joseph of the Carpenter Tribe, her father's friend. In his hand, she saw a lengthy staff upon which the butts of five sprigs still remained as knobs to fit his grasp. She wondered if it were a staff he always carried or a symbol that he, too, was a candidate for the choice of Halhul. Mary knew he was older than the other candidates, but time had touched him so lightly that its passing showed only in the nobleness of his brow and the wisdom deep within his eyes – calm, luminous eyes that suddenly flashed in her direction.

Quickly Mary looked away, but not before she sensed a strange gentleness in his steady gaze, a gentleness that wore a cloak of warm security. Such a feeling she had never known before, and so sweet it was she feared it should not be. She fought against its force by compelling herself to watch the priests as they gathered the staffs from the men. Her heart beat strangely as she saw a priest approach Joseph, hesitate uncertainly, then take his staff.

Up the altar steps the staffs were carried and back into the Holy Place. The seven priests returned to their original stations. Then Halhul strode solemnly across the connecting porch and disappeared through the curtained entrance to the Holy Place where the priests had left the gathered staffs.

The longer he was gone, the deeper the hush within the temple, until even the city noises beyond the wall were stilled as if all Earth paused to listen for a message from the sky. Mary's gaze moved across the sea of anxious faces and restless eyes. Again she saw Joseph. He seemed not to have moved, but still stood erect and quietly poised. Suddenly, his brilliant eyes flashed like the sun on a shining surface and turned toward the altar.

Halhul stood upon the balcony. In his hand was a staff. By its five sprig butts, Mary recognized it as Joseph's. Her throat hurt from the tumult in her heart. She was thrilled with awe as within her a strange conviction was born that behind these deeds of man the hand of God did move.

Halhul held the staff aloft and in vibrant, reverent tones announced, "When first I touched this staff, it was of dry, seasoned wood. Then before my eyes a bud of green appeared and burst into the blossom that you see. This is the sign for which I prayed and by its token he who brought this staff is chosen. And now the bearer of this staff will raise his hand."

From amid the crowd, frozen in stillness, Joseph slowly raised his hand. When it reached its fullest extension, a dove of purest white fluttered down from among the upper recesses of the temple and perched upon Joseph's head, its bright eyes and sleek neck moving back and forth as if in joyous affirmation of Halhul's selection. For a long moment, the people were hushed by this further sign. But soon their joy burst forth and upon Joseph was poured enthusiastic blessings from them all.

When the betrothal ceremony was over, Elizabeth walked with Mary as they returned to Mary's chamber. Never had the faces Mary passed seemed more familiar.

There were old, serene faces, middle-aged, uncertain faces, and young, eager faces. Faces she had seen each day for years. Faces that she might never see again. For the first time, she felt a keen affection for these faces – even though some had contributed to the unhappiness of her life. They were, after all, the only faces she knew. The old and familiar, no matter how uncomfortable, is always more dear and secure that the unfamiliar.

Today Mary was to leave the temple. For a short time she would be in her mother's home, for a princess must be married in the Royal home. Then she would go into a life that held naught but the strange, the new, the unfamiliar. Certain things would be expected of her, the nature of which she had heard in fragments. Her fancy enlarged the fragments, but she had no way of knowing how near to the truth she had arrived.

As Elizabeth and she crossed the huge Court of the Women, Mary looked about at its lofty splendor. For the first time it seemed friendly. The colors of the mosaics upon which she trod were warm and sympathetic. The marble column had lost their solemn dignity. The bubble of the fountain seemed a gurgle of contentment, and from the swaying evergreens came a peaceful, rhythmic murmur.

Mary was so overcome by the unexpected friendliness of it all that she hesitated. Elizabeth paused and looked quizzically back at her. Confusedly, Mary quickly resumed her pace.

Reaching Mary's chamber, they sat in silence. Upon Mary's finger was the ring with which Joseph had made his pledge. In her hand, she held the golden coin with which the pledge was sealed. Her eyes were on the coin,

symbol of the fact that the remainder of her life had been
pledged to this Joseph man.

Slowly, she placed the coin in a tiny box made of highly polished cedar from the hills of Lebanon. The box was
a betrothal gift from her father, who, smiling significantly,
had confided that it had been wrought by Joseph's hand.
Closing the lid, she turned the box in her fingers. Through
her window the rays of the afternoon sun revealed the perfect craftsmanship displayed in the delicate inlay.

She glanced across at Elizabeth who was watching with
silent understanding. Averting here eyes, and with difficulty, Mary questioned, "What manner of man is this
Joseph?"

Quietly, Elizabeth answered. "The man most fitting in
all the land to be your husband. The purest of heart, the
noblest of mind, the strongest of body."

Mary pondered her words, then continued. "Why have I
never seen him before? Throughout the years, he has never
stood among the multitudes and worshiped in the courts,
or I would have seen him."

"And if you had seen him," Elizabeth suggested with
gentle significance, "you would have remembered him?"
Without waiting for an answer, Elizabeth explained,
"Joseph objects to the rite of animal sacrifice. Therefore,
the law excludes him from the privilege of temple worship."

Something deep within Mary stirred. Many, many times
she had listened to the terrified bleating of little lambs as
they neared the scattered blood and burned flesh of their
own kind. And many times, she had gone to sleep to the
cooing of doves that at the next morning's worship would

be killed and burned. Many times as she lay awake listening to their gentle sounds, in the guarded depths of her heart, she had wondered if there were not less cruel ways of expressing adoration to Jehovah.

"Does this Joseph have any other strange convictions?"

Again Elizabeth nodded and Mary thought she caught a twinkle in her eyes that did not fit the solemnity of her bearing. "He does not accept the tyranny of wealth and will neither make, nor trade in, weapons which man can use in war; nor will he own or deal in slaves."

A sigh of something akin to relief trembled upon Mary's lips. Her inner being bore witness that all these things were right. "Are there others in the land who believe as he does?"

Elizabeth nodded. "Many," she said softly.

No wonder she had never seen him before, Mary thought. Part of his convictions were contrary to the Jewish law and another part contrary to the law of the Romans. The Temple had enough conflict with the Palace without borrowing more through imprudent sympathies or affiliations.

Smiling, Elizabeth announced lightly, "Zacharias and Joseph are very close friends."

"Yes?" Mary encouraged.

"They admire each other very much, but their beliefs are so opposite that when they are together it is amusing to note the careful path their talk treads in order not to crush the other's toes."

Mary smiled, but this friendship between Joseph and Zacharias brought to mind a question that still filled her anxious heart. A question her maidenhood did ask, but found difficult to utter, even to the understanding counsel of her kin and friend. But ask she must, so with difficulty she made a start. "Is it not dangerous," she murmured, "that my husband should be of my father's generation? I have devoted my life to preparation for motherhood. I understand but little of these matters, but I am aware that often barrenness results from unions wherein the span of ages is so wide."

Elizabeth realized how difficult it had been for Mary to ask this question and prepared herself to phrase the answer with care. She arose and walked to the table laden with betrothal gifts from which she selected a string of beads of many colors. She pulled their cool, round smoothness thoughtfully through her fingers, then laid them across Mary's folded hands.

"Each bead," she said, "might be of different color, or come from different clime or time. But each is held within its place and sequence by the string. Changing tides of circumstance can cause part of it, or the whole, to move, just as I moved the beads, in part, through my fingers and then handed the string as a whole to you. But the sequence of the beads remains the same.

"In such manner are people's lives strung together. He who strings the beads has a purpose to fulfill. The age of one, the color of another, these were all considered in the making of his plan. A single bead that could break and crumble would not be used because this would bring to naught the purpose of the whole. And he who planned this string knew well the strengths of his materials."

Reaching over and touching one of the beads, she continued. "This bead is Mary. The next Joseph. Perhaps, I am one of the others, and still another my son to come. Who knows? But I do know that every bead in the string will be found sufficient to carry out the purpose for which they all were strung! Does this answer your question, my child?"

In reply, Mary took her hand, kissed it, and held it to her cheek. She felt weak and small, like a birdling whose wings are caught in a strong wind of purpose. Her life stretched forth as a winding, unknown trail. She would leave the familiar life in the temple. New and strange duties would fill each day. But in the secrecy of her heart was a shield against all fears of the unknown. The shield of her covenant with the sun. The sun had said she could bring into this world a man so strong in the power of love that even death would be defied. Somewhere along the unknown trail that lay ahead this wondrous thing could be. She knew not where or how, but he who strung the beads would know.

And then there was this Joseph man. She could still feel the strength of him as he stood by her side at the betrothal ceremony. So, with the sun, the stringer of the beads, and Joseph, she felt she had all the help anyone could need. As ever, her greatest fear was that within herself could be found the weak link of the chain.

Still holding Elizabeth's hand, she spoke. "Without your love and wisdom upon which to lean, this would have been a day of terror. Now I can go forth to my task with confidence. When first I feel in me the life of him of whom the prophets speak, I will straightway come to you so that together we may share the joy of the things to come!"

Standing at her side, Elizabeth looked down. Wistful was her smile. Solemn were her words. "In the things to come, our part will truly be a woman's part. For we shall share joy only as we discover the *purpose hidden in pain.*"

CHAPTER 4

When Mary was prepared to leave, Halhul convened all the temple women. Standing at his side, Mary watched as they approached from all sides of the court. No longer did she fear to leave the temple. Elizabeth's story of the string of beads had awakened courage and confidence. Now she welcomed the challenge of the unfamiliar.

Presently, she would leave behind the loneliness and isolation she had endured. What was more important, she told herself, she would be free from the cause of her resentment. The life in which it existed would now be exchanged for a new one.

She stole a glance at Zaele, the girl she had surprised at the pool and who had provoked in her such a terrifying emotion. Zaele's arrogant smugness as she waited with amused indulgence for whatever additional ceremony must be endured on Mary's behalf caused a little hard-knotted feeling in the pit of Mary's stomach. She felt the heat of resentment crawling up her neck.

Quickly, she looked away. Oh, how grateful she was that today Zaele would pass out of her life! How wonderful to be free of her. Mary wondered what this last gathering was for and wished Halhul would quickly have done with it.

Lifting his hands for silence, Halhul spoke. "It is the time and year when the weaving of another Temple Veil is due."

Mary wondered what this could have to do with her. The Temple Veil hung between the Holy Place and the Holy of Holies and none but the High Priest ever passed beyond its folds on the day of Atonement. In the Holy of Holies was the Ark, with its mercy seat, and in the outer Holy Place were the altar of incense, table of shew bread, and golden candlestick used for the daily service.

"Today Mary leaves the temple," Halhul continued. "In accordance with the prophets, five handmaidens shall accompany her. Mary and the maidens will take the sacrificial wool and from it spin the threads with which the Veil is to be woven. The threads of purple will be spun by Mary's hand. The other colors will be spun by the maidens who accompany her. Those whose names I now call will be the ones to go: Saphora, Rebecca, Susanna, Abigea, and Zaele."

Mary's senses reeled. Zaele was to be one of her handmaidens! The temptation from which she thought she would be free was to be closer than ever! Suddenly, she was weak and afraid. Why must this be? Had she not suffered enough at the hands of this girl and her associates without having a closer association thrust upon her?

In her inner panic, she glanced about as a frightened animal seeking escape. Her glance swept over the descending steps toward the western gate of Coponius and the outside world. There it fastened itself.

The inner side of the walls were draped in the afternoon shadows. The sun had reached a point in its westward journey where its rays completely filled the arch of the gate of Coponius. In the midst of shadows, this arched gateway was filled with brilliant, vibrant light. Mary interpreted it as a beckoning door of light, the sun, her friend and counselor, pointing the way through a path of shadows. Vibrating in the archway, she saw these words: "Be not afraid. I will light the way and there will be strength when strength is needed."

Outside the gate a caravan of camels waited, their rich trappings and coat of arms indicating that they belonged to the House of David. Joseph, Anna, and Joachim waited with the caravan. Presently, Mary and the maidens came through the gate. The single-humped camels were made to lower their saddle litters so that the passengers could climb into basket-like compartments lined with cushions and covered with awnings.

Through the gate, five priests came bearing the sacrificial wool from which was to be spun the thread to weave the new veil. When this had been loaded into a saddle-pack, the caravan began its journey through the streets of Jerusalem toward the Damascus Gate at the northwest wall of the city.

Joseph, on a huge, powerful camel, led the way. Mary's camel followed. Then came the maidens, two in one litter and three in another. Behind them were Mary's mother and father. Bringing up the rear were several camels laden with tents and supplies, attendants walking at their sides.

Mary experienced a new lightness of heart as the procession moved through David Street, a narrow, winding opening between over-hanging walls that had resounded to so many different sounds – songs of triumph, yells of battle rage, moans of despair, murmurs of hope, cries of anguish, bursts of laughter, and the blessings of pious priests. To her, it was the passageway into a new life, a new world.

Mary was thrilled, even though in the litter behind her,

in the person of Zaele, she carried into her new world a
personification of all that was unpleasant in the old.
Turning her head slightly, she glanced at Zaele. Zaele's
eyes were fastened upon Joseph in feminine appraisal and
speculation. Mary felt a new concern in regard to Zaele.

The constant cloud of dust, the exasperating deliberate-
ness of other beasts of burden as they moved aside to
allow the caravan to pass, only added zest to Mary's new
adventure. The exuberance of her youth, the sensitiveness
of her reactions, and the strength of her spirit responded to
the stir and color of the crowded shops. Each scene
aroused new excitement. From now on, she would also be
part of this outside world.

Across their path ran a white sow followed by a litter
of pink pigs twinkling in the sun. Mary laughed in sheer
delight at the sight of them. Turning in her seat, she stared
at an Arab holding a young gazelle in his arms, fascinated
by the bright softness of its eyes. When she again faced in
the direction she was going, she caught Joseph smiling at
her. In his fleeting smile was the same gentle understanding she had seen before. As if he had fathomed her very
thoughts and would patiently stand by while she became
accustomed to the unfamiliar outside world.

The bronzed people in flowing garments of many colors, the grotesque camels under various trappings and bur-
dens, the flocks of flat-tailed sheep and lop-eared goats,
the shallow curiosity of the people, the brilliant fronts of
the shops extending back into mysteriously dark interiors;
all these things kept her eyes busy, eyes that had been so
long within temple walls. However, something kept her
from losing herself completely in the fascinating spell of
this new world – a vague feeling that the attractive colors,

noises and motions of her new world must always be but passing scenes in her journey. To have, but not to hold; to be of, but not in. Together with this feeling was a warning that hidden within the beckoning scenes were briars to snare and scratch her feet if she tarried on her journey.

Her young mind and heart neither clearly understood the threat of this new world, nor the promise of the complete journey. With a little shrug of impatience, she attempted to throw off the weight of purpose that had rested so long and heavily on her young shoulders, shoulders that at this moment were erect and eager. Suddenly, Mary made a discovery. She found that at regular intervals her eyes returned from the attractions of the passing panorama to the back of Joseph's neck.

"Why," she asked herself, "do I do that?"

In an honest effort to answer herself, she consciously studied the back of Joseph's neck. After a while, she decided it was because, no matter what the motion of the camel, the dignity of his bearing remained the same. His shoulders were broad, lean, and square; and rising from their squareness, his neck was smooth and strong. Mary saw now that the reason his neck caught her eyes was that it always held Joseph's head at the same angle. Regardless of the sway, Joseph's head seemed to be independent of its motion. The rest of his body moved in rhythm, but his head maintained at all times a certain posture. In his carriage was the dignity of dominion, dominion over all motion.

Mary wondered why she had not noticed it before. Perhaps it was not so obvious. If it had been, there would have been more arrogance than authority in his manner. That is what it was – authority over himself and over all with whom he came in contact. Something stirred deep within her as she again sensed the subtle strength of this man with whom she was to live and to share this new adventure in living.

She felt no fear or anxiety about this authority. It seemed to spring from a state of being. Most authority she had encountered came from possessions or a state of office, but his authority came from a state of *being*. The strength of his dominion lay in his poised stillness. When again she returned her attention to the passing scenes their fascination had strangely faded.

At the junction of David Street and the street leading to the Damascus Gate, they encountered a tense traffic congestion. The caravan of a rich merchant was entering David Street from the Damascus Gate. Ahead of the caravan came several burly men with prodding poles savagely clearing the narrow street so that their caravan could come through.

A very small, aged woman with her meager flock of sheep was caught in the path of those making way for the caravan. Her sheep were scattered in terror by the cruel proddings of the poles. The woman herself was so roughly brushed aside that she fell in a heap against a shop front.

Joseph quickly turned his huge camel sideways, blocking the street. One of the advancing prodders was against Joseph's camel before he recognized the royal trappings of the obstructing caravan. Leaning over, Joseph snatched the pole from the man and prodded him in the chest with it so hard that he was thrown heavily to the street.

Holding the pole firmly against the man's middle, Joseph began to twist. The pole caught in the man's clothes. Harder and harder Joseph twisted. Tighter and tighter wound the clothes, until so tightly wound were they that by using his camel's back as a lever, Joseph was able to raise him into the air at the other end of the pole. Holding the now screaming, squirming man aloft at the end of his own prodding pole, Joseph sat calmly upon his camel, blocking any traffic coming from the direction of the merchant's caravan. The other men, on seeing how one of their prodding poles had been quickly used, disappeared in the direction from which they had come.

Still holding the man aloft, Joseph turned toward the little old woman who had now gained her feet. Gently, he instructed, "Shepherdess, gather your sheep and go your way."

The shepherdess moved to do Joseph's bidding. As she passed near him, she looked up. Mary could see her upturned face and was astonished at its brightness and poise. She heard these words from the little shepherdess as she passed. "The day will come, Joseph, son of David, when I will repay you for this noble deed."

Mary saw astonishment momentarily sweep across Joseph's face. Smiling to himself, he glanced penetratingly once more at the strange little shepherdess; then with a mighty heave, he tossed aside the man and the pole and signaled for his own caravan to proceed.

Joseph's manner did not indicate that anything unusual had happened. But to Mary, a new side to her betrothed had been revealed. She had been spellbound by Joseph's unexpected actions. She had witnessed both his strength and his gentleness. Now she knew they both extended into the other. His strength was used for gentleness and his gentleness drew on a tremendous strength.

The royal trappings of the House of David, plus

Joseph's demonstration of his contempt for the merchant's
tyranny were sufficient to ensure their unhindered progress
through the street. Near the Damascus Gate they passed
the merchant's caravan, now stopped and off to one side to
permit their passing. Standing near the caravan was the
merchant himself, profusely bowing with respect and fear.

Outside the gate they paused briefly in an immense
olive grove. The attendants moved from one camel to
another, checking the loads and harnesses against the
strain of the forthcoming journey.

Leaving the city walls behind, they moved northwest
toward the rolling hills of Galilee. With mixed feelings,
Mary turned for a farewell sight of Jerusalem. It was
crouched in the setting sun, tense with terrific vitality.
Mary felt a vague fear of its impersonal strength, sensed
that her life would some day feel its force. She knew not
how nor why, but something within her resisted this vitality, this restless force straining subtly at an invisible leash.

She let her gaze wander over the brown battlements,
white-washed houses, flat roofs, slender minarets, many-
colored domes reflecting the sun with different degrees of
brilliance, and towering above all the temple and the
palace. The temple and the palace, each apparently seeking to dominate the city, yet realizing that as long as the
other existed this could not be, and because of this realization, seemed to smile diplomatically at each other. One
last look – and then Mary turned her face toward their des-
tination.

They passed through valleys and level plains, the fields
green with wheat and barley and watered by streams
descending from the Wadi Farah. Along the road grew bal-
sam trees and thorny jujubes, the latter laden with sweet,

insipid fruit. An occasional splash of color from blood-red poppies raised Mary's spirits.

They wound upward past herds of patient cattle and flocks of busy goats. The timid sheep were herded away from the dangers of the highway. The goats always furnished amusement. Some stood on their hind legs, browsing on the foliage of scrub oak; some showed off in butting contests atop a pile of rocks or a cleft along the road, while others with obvious disdain for such behavior sedately pattered along with as much dignity as flapping ears would permit. Eastward behind the hills, Mary could trace the long, vast trench of the Jordan valley, running due north and south, filled with a thin, violet haze and terminating in a glint from the Salt Sea.

At two instances, her eyes met Joseph's and between them flashed a warmth of understanding that swelled her heart with hope for the quality of their coming relationship. One instance was when over a hill floated the high pitched quavering voice of a shepherd singing to his flock; and the other was when a fawn-gray partridge, glistening red and black about the head, clucked like a hen for her scattered brood before whirring away in a low, straight flight, only to circle and return to the same spot where she had left her deserted chicks. This hope for a special relationship she hugged with feminine anxiety. The quality of the relationship between man and woman, she felt, depended upon the quality of their interests. She had noticed a brightness lurking in Joseph's eyes, as though waiting to illuminate his smile in appreciation of that which caught his interest.

From the quality of that at which she had seen him smile, she knew this brightness was often brought into

play, because, with a lavish hand had been placed in the
world those things at which he smiled, but only to a wise
and understanding heart were they revealed. Such things
as the maternal concern of the partridge hen and the love
for his flock in the shepherd's lilting song.

All the things Elizabeth had told her of this strangely
strong man came back to her. Mary felt that his strength
was not only of the worldly kind, but also came from his
ability to see through and behind the world. Her eyes suddenly filled with tears of gratitude for the security of such
strength. She clutched the swaying sides of her litter to
steady herself, whispering a prayer of thankfulness.

In a little grove, sheltered against the winds from
across the Jordan Valley and plentifully supplied with
water from a spring, Joseph halted the caravan for the
night. The attendants unloaded the camels and erected the
tents while Mary's mother, Anna, supervised the preparation of their evening meal.

When the fire of dry wood had produced sufficient
coals and ash for baking, little disks of meal and oil were
put on to bake. At the proper time, they were turned and
the result was a crisply delicious ash-cake. These cakes
spread with honey comprised the main dish. The simple
fare was augmented by cucumbers, figs, olives, raisins,
and pistachio nuts.

This was the first meal of her new life, Mary realized
as she gazed around her into the silent faces reflecting the
flickering firelight. She looked at her mother, so patient in
her fatigue; at her father, his eyes still bright with pride
and excitement; at the maidens, prim and a bit perplexed
as to what was expected of them; and then at Joseph,
poised in his still strength, quietly carving a little figure

from a piece of wood. She told herself that all of these people had been brought together at this particular spot as part of the plan of which she was the central figure. Her mother's fatigue, her father's pride, the maidens' perplexity, and Joseph's strength were all offerings on the altar of what was expected of her.

The fitfully burning fire, fanned by a playful breeze that found its way around the sheltering hill, caused everything to dance with eerie lights and shadows. Just when Mary was beginning to question the reality of herself and everything else, Anna arose from the fire, a signal for all to retire to their respective tents for the night. Mary followed, conscious at every step of Joseph's awareness of her, although he only nodded without looking up from his carving.

CHAPTER 5

Rediscovering the ancestral home of her birth was an experience that absorbed Mary's interest for several days. It was located in the little town of Saffuriyeh, just below Nazareth. The building was foursquare with a great vaulted height of finely hewn stone standing since the reign of David when it was built as a retreat from summer heat. Heavy roofed arches rested on massive marble pillars; the high ceilings and thick walls afforded a pleasantly even temperature. Floors were overlaid with cool marble and walls were covered with smooth plaster, some of which were tinted with shades of vermilion. The rooms enclosed a large court surrounded by cloisters and galleries. In the midst of a landscape of cypresses and olive trees bordered by a hedge of cacti was a well with water that remained sweet and cool from generation to generation.

Encircling the outside entrance to the house was a forecourt from which stairs of exquisitely carved wood led to the roof. In a secluded corner of the roof, Mary found that part of the house that she secretly claimed as hers. Here all her pent-up emotion could be released into outward expression and all the beauty and significance of the outside world could be assimilated within.

Here was one of the loveliest views of all Palestine. She suspected the house location had been selected because of the view. Westward, in a gradual color-changing descent to the Mediterranean, rolled the plain of

Esdraelon. Stretching southward, it dipped into the Valley of Jezreel. Far below, at a distant crossroad, Mary could see creeping caravans of Arabian merchants, glittering legions of Roman soldiers marching along the highway, and ever-present files of Jewish pilgrims moving along all roads leading to Jerusalem.

To the north, snug against the side of lofty Jabel Jermak, gleamed the city of Safed. Directly behind her and slightly above, terraced on the shoulder of a prominent Galilean hill, was the town of Nazareth. Stretching in between were undulating grassy knolls, interspersed with blossoms of delicate pink flax, golden chrysanthemums, and blue campanulas.

As Mary's eyes rested upon an imposing house in Nazareth that belonged to the Prince of the Carpenter Tribe, her heart lifted with warm excitement. The flowers blooming on the hillside between where she stood and this house on Marmion Way in Nazareth seemed to form a bridal path. Soon the wedding festival would take place and then, led by her husband, she would walk through the gentle beauty of these flowers to be presented to the House of the Prince of the Carpenter Tribe.

Try as she might, Mary could never look upon Joseph's house without experiencing tightness in her throat and subdued excitement in her heart. She couldn't determine whether the excitement was due to her coming personal relationship with Joseph or to the house as the setting where the real drama of her life was to be enacted. In either event, the house itself was a very important entity, which at one time beckoned with warm friendliness and, at another time, frowned forbiddingly.

Busy days passed. Every afternoon Mary and the maid-

ens gathered at the cooler north end of the enclosed court
to spin the wool into yarns from which the Temple Veil
would be woven. Gradually, in such close companionship
and by conscious effort on her part, Mary broke down the
reserve of the other maidens. They began to spontaneously
include her in their conversations, where before there had
been only studied courtesy toward her.

All but Zaele. She continued to be a thorn in Mary's
side. Hardly a day went by but that the old resentment she
had fought in the temple was in some way rekindled.
Instead of being freed from it when she left the temple, it
came along with her and its recurrence was becoming of
grave significance to Mary. To be capable of this feeling
of resentment while in the temple had been bad enough,
but to bring it with her into the sanctuary of her own home
and toward a guest within its walls was far worse.

The wedding festivities were only a few days distant.
The girls spent every moment free from their duties in
making dresses they would wear when the crowds arrived
for the ceremony. The bringing together of young men and
women at one wedding festival usually resulted in other
weddings. Consequently, the skirts and blouses and shawls
were receiving much attention.

A sense of competition was inevitable. Alone and in
pairs, the girls secretly prepared their costumes to suit
their individual charms. Though still temple maidens, at
age fourteen they could decide whether or not they would
spend the remainder of their lives in the temple. Many
things might happen at a festival and it was wise to be prepared.

One afternoon Mary felt a strange depression. Unable
to throw it off, she decided to go to the roof and see if

solitude and nearness to the sky would help. As she stood in her special spot gazing across the westward rolling plains, she heard voices and giggles. Her attention was arrested because she had always considered her roof retreat sufficiently removed from house sounds. She discovered that the sounds were coming from a corner of the inner court below where she stood. She recognized Zaele's low resonant voice and the admiring titter of Rebecca, a negative, colorless girl who was attracted to Zaele's vitality and physical beauty. It was natural they would pair off together.

"Wait until they see this!" Zaele said triumphantly. Rebecca's answering giggle of approval was a little uncertain.

Mary could not see to what Zaele referred, but sense it must have something to do with the wedding she had been working on for several days. However, that which came next drove all speculation from her mind.

"They will see!" Zaele continued. "I will have a husband! A rich one, too! And I will not need to own all the land in Palestine to do it!" A quality of contempt crept into her tone. "Neither will I need to have the old ones making prophecies about my giving birth to a Messiah!"

Rebecca's answering snicker was faint and half-frightened at such a daring statement.

"One is expected to believe anything," Zaele scoffed. "It is even whispered that old Elizabeth is with child and a holy one at that! But I do not believe it. Neither do I believe Mary is to be mother of a Messiah. The purpose of this wedding is to unite the wealth of the two families of David."

Zaele laughed a hard, accusingly prophetic laugh and continued, "I know the desires of men. I am fourteen next month and I expect to go to a rich husband, not back to the temple for the remainder of my life!" Zaele's voice was guttural with in its intensity. "If it were not for her wealth and this absurd Messiah prophesy, Mary could not interest a man like Joseph. Let him have eyes for me and I would know how to cause his eyes to sweep and burn as the breath of Sherkiyeh blowing from the desert!"

Mary's senses reeled. This one girl had tried for years to poison her relationships with other temple girls, had sought to defame her publicly, had even hurt Elizabeth in many ways. And now did dare to plan to use her wiles and beauty to corrupt Joseph's wonderful manhood! Mary's entire being cried out against the injustice of Zaele's very existence. She was suddenly possessed of a furious desire to destroy this being who seemed interested in naught save the destruction of Mary and all that was noble and dear to her.

Turning, she rushed to the stairs, glancing wildly about for a weapon with which to attack this personification of vileness. From the top railing post of the stairs extended a slender, finely carved, wooden rod supporting a highly polished, heavy wooden ball. Mary broke this rod from the post. Thought of all else but to attack Zaele was driven from her mind. She was a different person, a stranger to herself, an entity created out of the frantic necessity to remove Zaele's influence from her life.

With her raised weapon grasped tightly, she descended the first step. Through the revolving haze of consciousness, Mary heard her name called. She descended two more steps before the voice penetrated far enough to be recognized. She stopped. Gripping the railing, her slender figure grew rigid.

It was the voice from the sun.

"Mary!" again came the voice.

Mary shook her head as if to remove from her ears the sound of the voice she loved so dearly. She would never again hear the voice. That which she was about to do removed her forever from its association and from all its association meant.

"Go away!" she muttered through clenched teeth. "I would destroy this person who is determined to destroy me and mine. Spare me the sound of your voice!" she pleaded. "I have failed you! Utterly and miserably have I failed you!"

In response to the drive of her anger she descended another step. "Though I have failed your purpose," she continued in desperate tones, "I still must punish this girl. She has taken my all, leaving naught to my life but a husk of rebellious resentment."

Again came the voice from the sun. "To be tempted is not a sign of weakness. Temptation is as close to humans as the air they breath. It is the substance of which their road is made and only over this road is progress made."

At the next step, Mary stopped as the voice continued. "Temptation provides grain for the mill of our will. It is the shield against which we test the strength of our sword, the cloth to which we apply the measuring rod of our wisdom. It supplies adventure to the divine conquest of living. Without temptation upon which to place our feet there would be no heights to climb."

Mary descended another step, then paused as the voice

persevered. "It is not expected that humans live without error, but they are expected to profit by their mistakes. Bring not forward the past to plague the future, but convert all experience into understanding."

Mary had reached the bottom step.

The voice seemed nearer and clearer. "Judgement belongs to the law of the universe. Vengeance is mine, says the Law of the Lord. When we judge others, as you are judging Zaele, we move in the domain that belongs to the Lord.

Judge not lest you be judged by the Law. Remember this, my child, to judge not is the only path to peace. See Zaele for what she is, a vigorous, young creature, caught in the snare of her zest for living. She is far more subject to temptation than you are. Through your own temptation, you should understand hers, not condemn it."

The voice suddenly became so gentle that Mary fell into a sobbing heap upon the bottom landing of the steps. The weapon dropped from her hand and rolled away.

The voice continued with infinite kindness. "Do not feel that all is ruined. Go forth from here as we planned. Judge Zaele no more for her transgressions. They are but weaknesses that the law will convert into strength!"

"I will try!" sobbed Mary. "I will try!"

CHAPTER 6

The marriage ceremony held in Mary's ancestral home was over. In the upper room, the betrothed pair had stood beneath a canopy as Halhul, high priest of the temple, finished the ritual he had begun in Jerusalem. The crowns Mary and Joseph wore had been exchanged several times. They had pledged each other in new wine, after which the marriage contract had been read and attested to by each person present in passing of the wine cup. Following this ceremony, their friends had walked around the canopy, chanting psalms and showering rice upon the couple, after which Halhul concluded the ritual by invoking the seven blessings upon them.

Night had arrived, the time for Joseph to lead her to his house up the hill, before Mary could bring any sense of reality into the day's activities. All her life she had looked forward to this ceremony, yet during the rites she felt so detached that she could hardly believe it was actually happening.

But now that she and Joseph stood outside the walls of her home awaiting the procession of friends and relatives who would accompany them to Joseph's house for the feast, her detachment dropped away and she was acutely conscious of several things.

She would never again enter her own home except as a guest. Henceforth the maintenance of Joseph's house and its traditions would be her responsibility. Also, she was

keenly aware of Joseph's presence. Once more she felt the
potency of his subtle strength. A gentle evening breeze
stirred his white robe, accentuating his tall, slender frame.
His dark eyes glowed in the soft lights of the stars.

Those who bore the hymeneal lamps arrived. Joseph
touched Mary's arm and over the soft grass of the rolling
hills they led the procession toward the ancestral home of
the Carpenter Tribe. The swinging lamps cast reeling
shafts of yellow light. Where their light penetrated the
darkness near her feet, Mary watched for one of the blossoms she had seen from the roof of her house. She knew
that most of them would have folded their delicate petals
for the night, but she wanted so desperately to see one
along the way. When she looked at them before, she saw
them as being there especially for her bridal path and she
felt she must see one. The farther she walked, the more
intent became her search until her desire became supersti-
tious in its intensity. It was an omen she sought.

She could feel Joseph's awareness of her distraction.
He slowed his pace and turned questioningly toward her,
but she continued her search. Suddenly, the lamplight
reflected a golden chrysanthemum directly in her path. As
she passed, its color and shape was a miniature sun shining through the darkness. With new enthusiasm, she quickened her step, confident she had seen her omen!

The house of Joseph, Prince of the Carpenter Tribe,
was similar to the house she had just left. Lighted lamps
bordered the huge enclosed court. Against one entire wall
was a table laden with food. From the other side of the
wide court came music.

The music thrilled Mary deeply. Never before had she
heard so many skilled musicians in one group. She stole a

glance at Joseph. He must have gathered them from far and wide out of consideration for her love of music. Even though he pretended to be interested in another direction, Mary knew he was watching her reaction to the musicians. A wave of warm appreciation swept over her. She had known he was strong, gentle, and wise, but now she knew he was thoughtful of her happiness as well. Much effort had been necessary to gather so many musicians.

She moved over, and standing in front of him, looked up into his face. "It makes me very happy," her voice was low and unsteady, "that the first words I speak to my husband are words of gratitude for his thoughtfulness. The music is glorious!"

Joseph smiled down at her without replying. She had never seen such a smile. His face scarcely moved, but tiny lights flashed in his eyes and then swarmed together to make a warm, mellow glow. He took her hand and led her to an elevated bench against the center wall between the feast table and the music. There they seated themselves, watching as the guests moved about the court.

Mary looked about at the happy, expectant faces. On a bench opposite her sat the aged, an expression of eagerness struggling through the dimness of their eyes. She knew within the house were rooms filled with babes and children. And milling in the court, in ever-increasing numbers, were the youths and the middle-aged.

The vests and veils of young women vied with the jackets and girdles of young men in embroidery and ornamentation. Beneath the strut of youth and the shyness of maid was an increasing holiday spontaneity and recklessness.

The musicians departed from the feast table and

returned to their instruments. There were hand-drums, ket-
tledrums, and tambourines; many types of flutes and various stringed instruments that included lyres and zithers.

The leader, a large man with a luxuriantly flowing
beard, approached the bench where Mary and Joseph sat.
Bowing low he spoke to Joseph. "Gracious host, it would
be a great honor if we could accompany your wife in
song."

Joseph turned to Mary.

Eagerly she accepted. The leader commanded silence.
In a warm, rich voice to the accompaniment of a well-
known folk melody, Mary sang one of her favorite songs
of David. "The Lord is my light and my salvation; whom
shall I fear? The Lord is the strength of my life; of whom
shall I be afraid?"

She resumed her seat, and after a moment of appropri-
ate silence, the music resumed in a more festive rhythm.
The psalm Mary had sung now had newer and clearer
meaning for her. She realized that that which she had
always feared – her own reactions – she feared no longer.
Deliberately, she thought of Zaele to test herself.
Sympathy was her only reaction. Great was Mary's joy.

Some of the people were beginning to move in harmony with the cadence and rhythm of the music. Dancing
was a personal expression, an interpretation of what the
music meant to the individual. Some merely swayed,
while others were more active in their interpretations.

In a far corner of the court, one dancer was attracting
much attention. At first Mary could not see through the
crowd, but as the dancer's abandon increased the crowd
spread out to allow more room. Presently, the dancer was

in front of Mary's bench.

It was Zaele! As Mary looked at the girl's costume, she instantly understood why she had mistaken the dancer for a man. Brazenly, Zaele had defied the modesty of women's mode of dress. Instead of a loosely fitting vest and skirt covered by a concealing robe, she wore no robe; her vest was body-tight and the seductive lines of her swaying hips were clearly revealed by the closely draped skirt.

A wave of pity arose in Mary as she watched Zaele. There was no element of criticism or judgment in her attitude, but rather an awakened understanding. In every motion and gesture of the dance, Mary could see Zaele's defiance of a world attempting to withhold happiness from her. Mary knew the purpose of the revealing costume was to display to the world the quality of physical charm Zaele could offer in return for that which she wanted, wanted with all the vigor of her frustrated femininity.

Mary's compassion increased as Zaele's dance continued. The spectators, having satisfied their curiosity, were careful not to show interest to a degree that might be suspected of approval. Mary glanced at Joseph. He was on the edge of his seat staring incredulously at Zaele's performance. A tremendous sigh of heavy reluctance shook his frame as he arose and signaled the musicians to cease playing. As master of the house, it was his duty to stop this young girl's ceremony of self-destruction, but judgment and punishment must come from the father or, in the case of this temple maid, from the high priest.

Halhul was on hand and he stepped forth from the stilled crowd. Having spent her emotion with the dance, Zaele stood frightened and bewildered at the unexpected result of her plans. Halhul's voice reverberated through the stilled court. "According to law, a woman who publicly exposes herself to attract a husband, becomes the property of the public and as such is ostracized. If a man then marries her, he shares her ostracism and is refused the privilege of temple worship!"

With each word, Zaele's brazen confidence visibly change to fear – frantic, desolate fear. Life had betrayed her. Spurring her on with the intensity of her desires, life had led her into a trap, there forsaking her. Deserted and defrauded, she awaited she knew not what.

The solemn resonance of Halhul's voice again accentuated the unnatural hush of the throng. "You have outraged the sanctity and dignity of woman's estate. Consequently, the privilege of woman's estate is denied you. Henceforth, the street shall be your home and if any man take you as his wife the gates of the temple will be closed to him!"

Zaele's dark eyes opened wide with horror. Frantically, she stared about like a wild animal at bay; then she crumpled into a hopeless heap, just a child lying in the center of the huge, silent crowd.

The pounding of Mary's heart was so violent it shook her chair. She could understand how Zaele's resentment toward her restricted life had grown until it became a thing alive, demanding to be reckoned with. Had not her own experience been similar? She touched Joseph's arm. He turned to her and deep within his luminous eyes, she saw pity for what was taking place. "Is there no other way?" she asked.

Slowly, Joseph shook his head and answered, "Only if the wife of a household should take her as a handmaid, assuming full responsibility for her conduct. That provision of the law is seldom used because wives hesitate to subject their husbands to the proximity of women who have been proven so unscrupulous. But since the law is for the protection of women, it also provides the possibility of women's clemency."

Deliberately, Mary recalled what Zaele had said she would do if Joseph should look at her. The memory stirred no resentment. She had no fear of Zaele's presence in her home. And what was most important to Mary, she felt no judgment toward Zaele for any of the things she had ever done.

Her fingers tightened on Joseph's arm and in a voice husky with sincerity, she asked, "May I bring this maid into your home? It was to accompany me that she was first sent from the temple and, in some way, I may be to blame for that which she has done."

Joseph only stared at her, nodding his assent, but his countenance was radiantly eloquent of the admiration he felt for this maiden wife of his.

Instantly, Mary stepped down from their pedestal seat. Hurrying to the huddled figure of Zaele, she lifted her to her feet. Zaele raised her head. Seeing Mary, her eyes widened with a new fear that Mary was, in some way, about to inflict well-earned vengeance upon her.

Mary's smile melted Zaele's fear and incredulity moved into her glazed, staring eyes. "Fear not and come with me!" Mary encouraged gently. Her arms about Zaele, she led her across the court toward the main part of the house. Zaele, her head upon's Mary's shoulder, wept in bewildered despair. The spellbound guests murmured in their astonishment.

It was the hour preceding dawn before Joseph accompanied Mary to her chamber in the woman's wing and departed to attend to his many duties as host. Her room was large and comfortable. Against one wall, between two latticed windows, stood a canopied bedstead. Through the latticed squares of the windows wafted the cool, fresh breath of a budding day. Hurriedly and gratefully, Mary accepted the invitation of her luxurious bed, snuggling deep into its crisp caress and encouraging her thoughts to review the significance and color of the preceding events.

Having put Zaele to bed and consoled her as much as anyone in her plight could be consoled, she had returned to her place beside Joseph. The emotional climax, witnessed by the people, held them in restraint for awhile. But soon the music overcame their caution and the festival reached a delightful height of enjoyment.

Now as Mary became aware of the strengthening dawn, she sensed in it a strangely palpable tenderness. Remembering the expression in Joseph's eyes as he left her, she wondered if the tenderness of the morn did not come from her own thoughts instead of through the windows. In either event, she was grateful for the gentle understanding of her splendid husband.

"Poor Zaele!" she sighed aloud and shuddered at the thought of her own battle with resentment, hoping her present victory was a permanent one.

With incredible clearness, she remembered Elizabeth's words on the subject. "Yes, my child," she had said. "the mother must indeed be found worthy. The quality of the mother's influence is the soil in which the seed is to grow. For, as a seedling, it is bound by that which binds all seedlings. Else its life would not demonstrate that which all seedlings are capable of attaining."

Suddenly, Mary's room was filled with a soft, yellow light! Light that streamed in vibrant shafts through the latticed windows. Quickly arising and grasping the latticework, she stared into the inflowing light. The upper tip of the sun was just visible over the hills of Galilee. From this glowing segment on the horizon, across the intervening space, came a gleaming golden cord of light, its pulsating length stretching from the sun's tip to Mary's room as though at those two terminals the golden cord was fastened.

The question Mary had been pondering when the light suddenly appeared was answered by a voice coming from within her room. "Fear not, Mary," it said, "for God has found you worthy!"

Trembling with awe, Mary released the lattice and prostrated herself humbly upon the floor. Always before the voice had come from the distant sun. Now it was in her very room. But it was not the same voice; a quality of infinite gentleness was missing. The voice spoke again. "Behold! I bring the light of the world which you shall conceive in your womb. When it is brought forth you shall call his name Jesus!

"He shall be great, the Son of the Highest and the Lord God shall give unto him the throne of his father David. And he shall reign over the House of Jacob forever and of his kingdom there shall be no end."

Infinite humbleness overwhelmed Mary. Her entire life had been directed toward this moment. Desperately, she desired that naught within herself be lacking. Meekly she asked, "How shall this be, seeing I know not man?"

Instantly the voice answered. "With God nothing is impossible. Your cousin Elizabeth conceived a son in her old age even though she was called barren! And this is the sixth month with her!"

Now Mary knew why the voice was different. This was not the voice from the sun, but that of the Angel Gabriel who had appeared to Zacharias. "The Holy Ghost shall come upon you, and the light of the highest shall over-shadow you, and this holy being that shall be born of you shall be called the Son of God. And this Son of God, being born as man, shall demonstrate man's dominion over life and death!"

Mary lifted herself to her knees and with her head still bowed in humbleness said, "Behold the handmaid of the Lord. Be it unto me according to your words!"

Then she felt the departure of Gabriel, but the light that he had brought remained within her room. Slowly, this light began to move. Around the room in a circle it moved, spinning faster and faster. As the light spun, the circle became smaller and brighter until it became an inverted golden cone suspended above Mary. Lower and lower descended the spinning, golden vortex. When the golden cone of light reached Mary, its outline disappeared and Mary was enveloped in light. She felt as though her being were composed of a myriad of tiny candles, all of which were suddenly lit. Upon the sweep of their combined flame, she seemed to soar higher and higher until she was swept into the realm of unconsciousness.

CHAPTER 7

M ary awakened in her bed. She did not remember
returning there from the floor. But this was insignificant compared to the change she discovered in herself.
The living, spinning cone of light now living in her body
so affected it that she was unconscious of weight. She felt
transparent, as fluid as the atmosphere. Light flowed
through her and she was light.

Enriched and revitalized, she also possessed new clarity
of vision. Clearness of understanding enabled her to see in
everything and everyone an affinity of purpose. This subtle integrity present in all life and form established in her
heart an unfathomable peace. Glancing at the window, she
judged it to be mid-morning. Suddenly, she wanted to look
upon the outside world with this new understanding, to see
the familiar through the eyes of her new and unfamiliar
self.

She would go to the roof. Hurriedly, she began dress-
ing. Here in her new home she would find another roof
sanctuary just as she had at the temple and in her mother's
home. Quietly, she made her way to the roof. The house
was still. No indication of the night's hilarity marred the
sparkling brilliance of the morning. A high, stone
balustrade rose above the roof's edge. At its eastern corner
she stood, her face as clear and bright as the world upon
which she looked. Eagerly, she drank in what she saw.
Within all lived a new beauty and meaning. The green
hills of Galilee, rolling away as far as she could see, gave

her a sense of friendly comfort. The white homes of
Nazareth, huddling together in neighboring clusters,
tugged sweetly at her heart.

All that she looked upon was an extension of herself.
She was part of it and it part of her. In this affinity of purpose was good, the result of the Creator's love for creation. Mary's being was aglow with the light living within
her. For an instant, the old fear returned. True, she had
been found worthy to bear this wondrous babe, but it
would be her responsibility to guide his growth through
childhood to manhood so that he would attain the heights
prophesied of him. Could she do it? Surely, all this divine
preparation could not be lost though her inadequacy as a
mother!

Shaking her head to remove such thoughts, she again
drank in the beautiful world spread out around her.
Someone moved in the court below. She recognized the
slender, dignified figure of Joseph as he inspected the
results of the night's activity. Mary was seized with an
impelling desire to share her glorious secret with him.
Gathering up her skirts, she raced down the steps and out
across the grassy court to him. He turned with perplexed
pleasure at her approach.

Her face shone so with joy of her tidings that Joseph
was astonished to see in her a quality of beauty that had
hitherto escaped him. "Compared to you, the brilliance of
the morning is dull and lifeless," he said, smiling down
into her beaming, upturned face.

"Oh, Joseph," she whispered rapturously, "I am with
child!"

Incredulous, he stared at Mary. The girl spoke with
amazing simplicity and directness. No woman was every

more proud, more free from shame! Could it be she did not know the significance of her announcement? Had the temple been so absorbed in sheltering her from minor transgressions that it failed to acquaint her with so serious an act? Searching her face, Joseph sought for some indication of shame, some plea for forgiveness, some petition for pity, a pretext or excuse. But he saw only pride and joy such as he had never seen before.

This grotesque turn of events assailing him so abruptly robbed him of reason. His mind was stunned, his heart anguished. Mumbling an excuse, he moved himself from her presence. Hurrying to the privacy of his chambers, he turned the wooden key in the huge door as though this act could lock away a suddenly distorted world. Pacing back and forth, he sought a possible explanation. It was obvious that his young wife felt she had done no wrong, for he had never seen a face more free from a sense of guilt. It must be that in her limited life in the temple, she had been uninformed of the attitude of the outside world toward such things. If he pointed out to her the extent of her transgression, he would first have to introduce to her a side and quality of life that for her did not exist.

A burning question clutched his wise and just heart as back and forth he strode. Suddenly, he stepped to the window, gripped the lattice and with eyes heavenward, cried aloud in anguish, "Which would be the greater sin on my part? To reveal the ugliness of life to a soul as fresh and clean as hers, merely for the privilege of pointing out her guilt, or to permit her to continue living in her present world? The purity of which is reflected by the brightness of her face!"

For hours, Joseph wrought with this question. Not until

the day was almost spent did he reach his decision. He would not expose Mary to herself! By living privately within his house, she could retain the beauty of her world and with a little effort on his part, she could be protected from the ugliness of the world.

Utterly exhausted, he threw himself upon his bed to sleep. Through the same window at which he had pled for an answer to his question, there suddenly streamed the rays of the setting sun. A Voice spoke in reassuring tones. "Joseph, son of David, fear not to take unto yourself Mary, your wife, for that which is conceived in her is of the Holy Ghost. She shall bring forth a son and you will call his name Jesus, for he shall save his people from their sins!"

The light faded. The voice ceased. Joseph sprang to his feet. He was afire with what he had heard. Never had he known greater joy. The prophecy of Isaiah was suddenly framed in his mind in flaming letters: "Behold, a virgin shall be with child and shall bring forth a son and they shall call his name Emmanuel, which being interpreted is, *God with us.*"

Why had he not thought of it before? Had it not been Mary's destiny from the beginning? And when it happened, she had hurried to him to share its holy significance. He had turned from her, leaving her alone. He had spent the day in weighing judgment against her for an imagined crime against his masculine pride. What could she have thought? Where was she now?

Groaning, repentant to the depths of his soul, he groped blindly for the key and threw wide the door. Stumbling across the court, he ran up the stairs to the door of Mary's chamber. Hesitating but an instant, he pushed open the door and hurried to her side. Seeing her lying there safe, he was overcome with relief and self-condemnation.

He dropped to his knees and rested his head upon her bed. His voice was hoarse with anguish. "Holy Mother, forgive me. Henceforth, my life will be lived for you. Blessed am I to be husband to you and your Holy Son!"

Mary's hands touched his head, her voice low with joy and gladness. "Blessed are we to have you for our husband and father!"

As the days passed, Mary grew in understanding as a rose unfolds its petals, a flower evolving toward the time when its perfume would enrich a waiting world with divine fragrance.

More and more, she became aware of her tremendous task. Her son must be so guided in the beginning of his earthly life that no human frailties would blight his divine fruition. He must grow from infancy to maturity; must go through he same trials and limitations as all men. How else could he experience man's lower self? In no other way could he test the fetters of the flesh. If he were not subjected to the temptations of human nature, how could he overcome that which was temporal and free that which is eternal? It was Mary's task to guide him until that which was infinite penetrated that which was finite – until the seedling pushing through the soil came into the light of the sun.

The magnitude of such a great responsibility appalled Mary and, at time, the strange profundity of her thoughts frightened her. She hungered for the comforting presence of Elizabeth. She had promised that when first she felt life within her, she would go to Elizabeth, so she decided to ask Joseph for his permission.

"Joseph," she said, "at this time, I desire the companionship of my cousin Elizabeth and she might have need of me. I beg your permission to journey to her home in Hebron."

Joseph nodded with quiet understanding. "Preparations will be made at once." Turning to depart, he paused and with obvious difficulty asked, "Is it your wish to go alone?"

The only reply he received was a look of sweet disapproval for such an unwonted suggestion that sped him on to see that the preparations were speedily and happily made.

When the caravan was ready, Mary noted that there were two extra pack camels besides the usual one for each traveler. Joseph observed her look of mild astonishment and quickly busied himself with the trappings. Mary's heart sang as she ascended into her litter, for she knew the extra camels were laden with Joseph's conception of what might add to comfort along the journey.

Leisurely, they descended the hills of Galilee and, before nightfall, pitched their tents near Jacob's Well at the mouth of the Shechem Valley. Reclining on several rugs carefully piled by Joseph beneath the flap of her tent, Mary, having finished her evening meal, watched the changing colors of the setting sun move across Mt. Gerizim, sacred mountain of the Samaritans.

Long ago, upon that mountain the Samaritans had built their temple of worship. A hundred years before Mary's time, the Jews had climbed the mount and destroyed the Samaritan's temple. Mary mused on the futility of man constantly destroying the symbol of another's faith. With her new power of insight, she understood it was man's lack of confidence in his own faith that cause him to destroy the evidence of another's faith; fear that the other's might be more potent than his own.

The next afternoon, the caravan passed through the Damascus Gate and entered the City of Jerusalem. They made their way to the ancestral home of Mary's father. There they were greeted by Anna and Joachim who were spending a few weeks in the city.

Leaving Joseph with her parents, Mary departed for the temple, the imposing edifice in which she had spent so many impressionable years. She was astonished to find that the steps she now climbed were just highly polished slabs of marble and the towering columns and lofty ceilings were but magnificent masonry. It was incredible that this had been the background of such unhappiness; that its previous significance had weighed so heavily upon the limited perspective of her youth. She had thought today's mission would be attended by hesitation and misgivings, but she felt not a single qualm.

For days she had watched Zaele's changing attitude and, from her own experience, she knew that such changes were possible. Zaele should not be condemned for the rest of her life because of an adolescent indiscretion. The stream of her life was exceedingly strong. In her youth, the guiding banks were indefinite and unstable. Because the stream once over-ran its banks, its force should not forever be doomed to the lonely wastes of the desert!

Halhul's old eyes shone with pleasure at the sigh of Mary as he observed the obvious changes wrought in her. However, his manner became reserved and cautious when Mary mentioned Zaele. "She harmed no one," Mary insisted. "She is guilty of naught but permitting the gushing fountain of her youth to spill its waters into certain pools, pools over which the tradition of humankind has placed the sign of pollution."

Mary touched the sleeve of Halhul's sacred robe and gazed earnestly into his face. "The fountain of her life still flows and the real guilt will lie with those who, in their judgment, say that naught but impure waters can come from this fount."

For a long moment, Halhul thought in silence, then a deep sigh stirred the majesty of his beard. "Such wisdom is as pure as the light in your eyes. The guidance of her life was in the keeping of the temple – therefore, the guilt lies with us."

Mary smiled her gratitude. "I hoped you would permit her to return, for even though she has not expressed this wish, I feel it is her desire."

As Mary left the pious patriarch, she felt his eyes seeking the reason for the change he found in her. Today, he saw a woman, wise in the ways of the world, but who a few weeks before was an inexperienced temple maid. But Mary felt that even from him must be kept the secret until her time was come.

As she left the temple, her secret of secrets, her trysts with the sun, weighed upon her with a new degree of intensity. It was one thing to give birth to this man who, according to the prophets, was to receive the throne of David, reign over the house of Jacob, and free the Jews from their enemies; but it was another thing to give birth to him who would overcome death. Never before in the history of her people had this been done by man.

She forced herself to stop and look at this human creature, passing to and fro. For the first time, she felt as a witness to life's activity, an impersonal bystander. All who passed indicated by their manner that they moved toward some purpose, their faces reflecting an anxiety over the outcome of this purpose.

Once Mary had seen a caged lion. She never forgot its constant, restless pacing to and fro within the confines of its cage – pacing that took it nowhere. Mary knew now that the lion had paced because of an undeniable urge for motion and, even though it got nowhere, this fundamental urge had to be satisfied. Thus, the lion had attained a limited measure of peace within his environment.

The throngs she passed now paced within cages made of various desires. Frantically, individuals moved toward desires, only to have the desires change before their very eyes, sending them off just as frantically in new directions. Because the desires were always changing, there could be no rest from the seeking. So the only difference between a human and the lion was the size of the cage. Both were satisfying the divine urge to grow, to develop, to evolve; appeasing the urge, but not accomplishing that for which the urge existed.

No longer did these new experiences in thought and understanding disturb Mary. It was as if such things had always been known to her, but, heretofore, had been hidden in another room of her mind, a room into which she had now entered through the door of that which lived within her womb.

Reaching the entrance to her mother's home, she paused atop the steps and, with pity in her heart, turned once more toward the throngs hurrying back and forth the cages of changing desires. "There is no one to show them

the way out of their cages," she murmured to herself. And
then answering herself, she said with a strange conviction,
"My son shall be their way!"

Dawn of the next day found them crossing the head of
the deep valley of Hinnon, on the road to Bethlehem,
whose name means the city of bread, spiritual bread.
Throughout the valley were cultivated fields that appeared
as patches of varying shades of red interspersed with the
greens of mulberry, hawthorne, and fig trees. At mid-
morning, they rested at the Mar Elijas Well and, soon
thereafter, the double hill of Bethlehem came into view,
surrounded by gardens, olive orchards, green fields, and
pastures.

In front of a large inn, in the center of Bethlehem,
Joseph stopped the caravan. At sight of the building, Mary
thrilled from head to foot. Though she had never seen it
before, she recognized it as the birthplace of David whose
throne her son was to inherit. It had become the home of
Boaz and when David became king, he built a fortress
over it. In course of time, it had become an inn, half of
which was endowed to entertain, without charge, teachers
and priests from other lands; the remaining half was leased
by Mary's family to another family who rented rooms to
the public for a livelihood.

As if reading her thoughts, Joseph announced, "At this
very spot, David was crowned King of the Shepherds. The
shepherds were so delighted that David was fair, a ruddy
child of the sun, that their songs of praise filled the heavens and they placed upon his golden curls a crown of spun
silver and wool."

Mary remembered the words of Samuel. "For he was
ruddy and fair and withal of beautiful countenance and

goodly to look upon."

The inn had a strangely magnetic attraction for her, a sweetly gentle, but insistent pull. Reluctantly, she left the inn behind as they set out on the last stage of their journey. For the remainder of the day, Mary daydreamed about the inn as David's birthplace and of the shepherds and their songs of joy. Occasionally, however, her attention would be claimed by the beauty of the passing country – the corn fields of Boaz, the bright green of almond trees, the dark green of carob trees, snowy blossoms of apricot, or the rosy bloom of peach trees. And as an overtone to it all came the friendly, mellow greetings of the meadow larks, heralding their approach to each new scene.

Toward evening, the trail wound up through wilder, rockier heights, leading past the great empty pools of Solomon, lying at the head of Wadi Artas. On the southern slopes of the heights, they made their camp beside one of the gushing springs of Wadi-al-Arrub, whose waters formed a laughing brook rushing at random through the valley below.

An early moon bathed the stilled earth in its soft light. Mary and Joseph reclined among their woven rugs and gazed out over the unfolded magic of the night. Upon a gentle breeze was borne to them the quavering notes of a shepherd's flute. Mary thrilled to the plaintive song and her reveries turned again to David and his shepherds. She settled deeper into her rugs. "Tell me more of this tribe of men called the Shepherds," she implored softly.

Joseph arose to throw a large, gnarled root upon the fire, then comfortably settled himself among his rugs to explain. "The calling of the Shepherds is a noble one. The owner of many herds is the prince, a priest, a shepherd of

men as well as sheep. He carries the Royal Crook, the
same emblem carried by Egyptian kings to indicate that
they were rulers of the two kingdoms of Egypt."

"Do not all shepherds carry a crook?" Mary asked.

"The common shepherd has a staff, but the staff has not
the royal crook. The prince divides his herds into flocks of
one hundred each and places them in the care of a shepherd. This shepherd names each of the sheep and talks to
them as though they were his children. He talks to the goat
that leads them and the dog that drives and protects them,
as though they were his brothers."

"Do the sheep, in turn, look to the shepherd as their
father?" Mary inquired hopefully.

Joseph nodded his head in solemn emphasis. "They
understand him and look to him for all their needs. They
know his voice and, if he calls, no matter how they may
be mixed up with other sheep in their grazing, they will
turn at once and come to him."

"Do many get lost?"

"Yes, but the shepherd seeks until the lost one is found.
When one is lost, the whole of the little flock mourns and
many will not eat until he is found." Mary noticed a growing huskiness in Joseph's voice as he continued. "It is
beautiful to see the joy of the ninety-nine when the lost
one is returned to them. The dog barks with joyous
approval and the goat, by leaping over the highest
promontories, shows that he, too, is happy."

Joseph became silent. For a long time, Mary refrained
from disturbing him. Then, with sincere concern, she
asked, "Those who grow old and weak must be killed?"

It was some time before Joseph answered. When he

did, there was hardness in his tone. "Only the little sacrificial lambs are killed."

Mary knew the unwonted harshness came from his intolerance of animal sacrifice and gladness stirred within her. When he spoke again, his voice resumed its normal gentleness. "Hunger he will endure before the shepherd will kill his sheep. In his own mouth does he chew the oil and meal and with it feed the ones that have become old and toothless. The same thing he does for the motherless lambs until they grow strong enough to graze.

"If blind, he brings them water in a cup running over. He leads the others to where he can dam the stream and provide for them a pool of still water."

"Why must this be done?" Mary asked.

"The nose of the sheep is long. If the water is rough, it gets into the sheep's nostrils. They are so timid they will not attempt to drink rough water."

"How wonderful," Mary sighed. "Is there more?"

Joseph smiled deeply. "Yes, if they are injured, the injured spot is rubbed with ointment. And in summer, if the heat is intense, to prevent sunstroke, the shepherd anoints their heads with oil."

A psalm of David's which began, "The Lord is my Shepherd, I shall not want," suddenly stood forth in Mary's mind. King of the Shepherds, David truly was! Only the King would have understood God's relation to man in terms of a shepherd. Mary's heart beat rapidly with new wonder. Her son was to inherit David's throne, to be King of the Shepherd Tribe. What a glorious heritage! This new understanding, brought to her by Joseph, contributed still another quality of significance to this life that lived within her.

   With deeper peace than she had ever experienced, she
stretched herself out to sleep. Just before sleep enfolded
her, she remembered that tomorrow she would see
Elizabeth. Anticipation spread a mantle of joy over the
depths of this new peace.

CHAPTER 8

Midmorning found Mary and Joseph approaching Hebron, oldest city in Palestine, and often called Abraham's Castle. Ascending its verdant vale, high enough above sea level to escape the destructive summer heat, they passed heavily fruited vineyards stretching as far as the eye could see. Much of this fertile land was of the house of Asher and, as such, belonged to Elizabeth and Zacharias.

Besides being the home of Elizabeth, Hebron held another significance for Mary. David had spent much time here – probably rode a magnificent charger over this same road her camel now trod with such resigned dignity. Twice here, David had been anointed King and for seven and a half years had reigned from Hebron as King of Judah. During this reign, six sons had been born to him, one of whom, Absalom, later chose this, his birthplace, as head-quarters for a rebellion.

An attendant at the gate of the outer court surrounding Elizabeth's magnificent home signaled their arrival to the household and immediately there followed the hurried patter of many feet in joyful preparation for their reception. Mary was stirred by a strange excitement. As was the custom, Elizabeth would wait to welcome her guests in the reception chamber. Mary pictured Elizabeth as last she saw her and wondered if it were possible that she had grown more glorious in grace and bearing. A surge of love and esteem for this wonderful woman, her cousin, swept over Mary and she was suddenly athirst for her presence. Their love for each other was now divinely sealed by the common purpose of the holy lives within their wombs.

Surrounded by many willing hands and bright, expectant faces, they dismounted within the court. Joseph approached Mary and the understanding within his smile that shone down upon her caused her to wonder if he had not felt her very thoughts. And when he spoke, she was certain of it. He said, "Go and greet Elizabeth. I must remain a while to attend my animals."

Mary marveled at the guilelessness in his noble face, for she knew the animals needed no more care than that provided by their attendants. With exquisite understanding for her feminine feelings, he was providing a private meeting for her and Elizabeth. Also, she knew, if Zacharias was home, Joseph would first be presented to him and Joseph would manage that their greeting be a lengthy one.

Servants stationed along the way, alert with courteous faces and interested eyes, indicated to Mary the direction where Elizabeth waited. At the end of a cool corridor, Mary descended several steps into a spacious reception room. Elizabeth stood in its center, her hands outstretched in sweet impatience. For an instant, Mary was stunned by the radiance of Elizabeth's countenance and recognized within its unearthly glow, the divine significance of the babe she was soon to bear.

"Peace, beloved cousin!" Mary whispered across the handsomely furnished room, now stilled with a palpable hush of expectancy.

At the sound of Mary's voice, Elizabeth painfully

clutched her side and was so faint she fell to her knees. But before Mary could reach her, Elizabeth released her side and still upon her knees held forth her arms and cried in a voice deep with joyous conviction. "Blessed are you among women and blessed is the fruit of your womb! At the sound of your voice, the babe in my womb leaped with joy!"

The sight of Elizabeth on her knees – Elizabeth, the wise and wonderful – caused Mary discomfort. Quickly, but gently, Mary lifted her to her feet and supporting her precious form with her abundant strength, led her to a rug-covered bench. There they sat in awed silence, each absorbed in the sheer sweetness of their reunion.

Elizabeth's shining eyes revealed the new glory she saw in Mary. She repeated in a significant whisper, "At the sound of your voice, my babe leaped with joy!"

Mary nodded, her tone was reverent as she said, "Yes, the two holy ones recognized each other's presence."

Elizabeth's incredulity at Mary's understanding was obvious. Seeing it, Mary said in a sweet, low voice, "Once you prophesied that all generations would call me blessed. Now that the Lord has made of me his handmaiden, thereby fulfilling your prophecy, why are you so astonished?"

Slowly and thoughtfully, Elizabeth answered. "It is one thing to prophesy, but another to witness its fulfillment. Prophecy is a gift, like the gift of sight; it is independent of one's control. Consequently, its fulfillment is just as surprising to me as to another." She laughed musically, declaring, "When last I saw you, I was the counselor and you the child; now it is I who am the child and you the counselor!"

They both laughed with strange elation. Then Mary said quietly, "We but lost the child and found another counselor; and, henceforth, counselors we must be since it was this role for which we were chosen – to guide our sons in the first steps of their journey across the stage of humanity's estate."

Nodding her head, Elizabeth added, "Through many lives, ours and others, were we prepared for this responsibility. And to a*ll life* are we obligated to discharge it wisely and faithfully."

For a few moments, they were both stilled by the significance of the lives within them. But such thoughts were too overwhelming to be prolonged. Soon they were chatting as two ordinary women about their husbands, Joseph and Zacharias.

The days passed pleasantly. Mary and Elizabeth were mostly alone, talking and making preparations for their approaching time. This left Joseph and Zacharias with the necessity of each other's entertainment. In the past, it had been impossible for them to be together very long without displaying the divergence of their feelings concerning the popular temple ceremony of animal sacrifice. Now that they were more closely associated than ever before, it was natural that their differences would be accentuated.

Zacharias could not speak so he sat at his writing table and wrote on the palimpsest. Joseph stood at his side that he might read what he wrote. If the ink were blotted while it was still wet, the same sheet could be used over and over again.

Each day, they would begin by Joseph chatting amiably about different subjects, his words designed, as much as possible, to enable Zacharias to answer with a gesture or a single written word. However, eventually, the question of animal sacrifice would filter through their studied avoidance and Joseph's words and Zacharias' quill would begin scratching at old wounds.

This particular morning found Zacharias almost violent in his resentment. He scratched so furiously that the blotting was forgotten and his papyrus supply threatened. The pen scratched spitefully in his clenched hand as he wrote, "Halhul must have been obsessed of Satan to choose a religious radical for the husband of our Messiah's mother!"

Though Joseph's face was pale and his eyes exceedingly bright, his manner was calm and deliberate.

Zacharias' pen scratched scornfully again. "A man who is not even permitted to enter the Temple any farther than the Gentiles' Court should not have been chosen as husband of the woman who is to bring forth the King of the Jews!" Throwing down his pen, he leaned back in his chair, shaking his splendid head in righteous indignation.

Joseph stepped around to where he could face Zacharias and declared bluntly, "Perhaps a radical was chosen that the might show this King of the Jews how to escape the quicksands of Jewish dogma. How could anyone caught in the brutal bigotry of your pomp and parade be aware of its diabolical effect upon the people? Much less do something about it! He would be as blinded as you!"

With fingers trembling with rage, Zacharias retrieved his pen and wrote, "Who are you to criticize our temple rites? You who have no temple in which to worship and whose religion is without history or record!"

Joseph read, then placing his hand upon his breast, replied, "My body is the only temple I need. Solomon's Temple, built without sound of hammer and saw. Within this temple, I feel the wings of my soul. In this temple, I worship the grace and beauty of our Creator's handiwork. Could there be more? The history of my religion is record- ed by humanity's progress along the path of Truth!"

Zacharias' bristling attitude subsided slightly. With obvious reluctance, he considered the substance of Joseph's words. Then, with apparent unwillingness, but driven by his deep-rooted honesty, he wrote, "In what way do you feel that we tread not this path?"

Joseph's face was alight with hope. He started to speak, hesitated, then gently removing the pen from Zacharias' hand, he leaned over the table and wrote upon the last sheet of papyrus, "In using the rite of animal sacrifice to enrich the temple treasury!"

Zacharias' defiance completely wilted. His proud, mag- nificent head lowered in contrition as he held forth his hand for the pen. With an unsteady hand he wrote under Joseph's words. "All my life I have fought just such a con- viction. I probably feared you were right – and that must have been why I always opposed you so vehemently." The pen fell from his fingers. He slumped listlessly in the chair, his patriarchal beard resting resignedly upon his deflated chest.

Joseph's eyes softened with understanding as he read the confession of this proud priest. He clasped the shoul- ders of his friend with sympathetic affection. Then quietly he left the room lest even a friendly presence make more bitter for Zacharias the utter capitulation of a life-long integrity.

Joseph entered the chamber where Mary and Elizabeth were busily spinning wool. He strode twice around the room before he noticed their questioning stares. He stopped and spoke in a pensive tone. "I have just seen honesty conquer pride!"

Joseph's gravity caused the women to grow tense with anxiety. A deep sigh shook his mighty frame as he explained. "Zacharias has just confessed that he sees no spiritual value in the rite of animal sacrifice!" He moved toward the door, paused, and from a melted heart, murmured, "Victory over one's friend is victory without savor."

When he had gone, the women looked long into each other's eyes. "Poor Zacharias," Mary said, "how his heart must have ached as his hand slew the lambs and doves."

In Elizabeth's eyes was fresh determination. Purposefully, she said, "The season of miracles is surely upon us. No time must we lose in preparing for the parts we are to play. Come with me."

She led Mary out of the house to a far corner of the court where they passed through a gate to another court of what once had been a magnificent dwelling. Now it was but crumbling brick and stone arranged in orderly, but meaningless, piles. Making her way through the masses of masonry, Elizabeth stopped at an ancient well from which occupants of this fallen house had obtained their water.

She looked about to make sure there were no spectators, then lifted the wooden well cover. A dark, yawning cavity gaped before them.

Mary stared apprehensively into the forbidding darkness of the opening, then inquired with concern, "What pray, are we to do here?"

In guarded tones, Elizabeth explained, "Beneath the sand at the bottom of this well is concealed a watertight door leading to a large chamber. In this crypt are stored objects that have been preserved by our people from generation to generation. These treasures are now needed by you and me."

Along one side of the well, in a precarious state of preservation, was a wooden ladder. Without hesitation Elizabeth descended, the ladder swaying and creaking under her weight. Mary's anxiety had become almost unbearable when at last the ladder again swayed and creaked. Mary dropped to her knees and attempted to steady it.

Finally, Elizabeth reappeared. Under one arm was a small, heavy, metal box. While still on the ancient ladder, Elizabeth held forth the box to Mary. Just as she clasped it, the rung upon which Elizabeth stood gave way. Elizabeth held on to the box for support while Mary frantically struggled to keep them both from tumbling into the well. Elizabeth's feet found the next rung and Mary pulled her up. For a moment, they stared at the box still clasped in their hands while they painfully regained their breath. Then they carefully recovered the well and hurried to the house. Mary was consumed with curiosity, but Elizabeth said not a word until they had regained the privacy of her chambers and the box was on a table and Mary was seated beside it.

The bronze hasps of the box were elaborately designed

and fashioned by an ancient artificer; age had not affected
the careful fittings and they yielded easily to Elizabeth's
efforts. A musty, spicy aroma quickly pervaded the room.

Elizabeth removed from the box several neatly folded
cloths. To Mary's astonishment and delight, they proved to
be swaddling clothes for infants. Holding them up for
Mary to see, Elizabeth announced with shining eyes, "The
real history of our people is written in the pattern of our
embroidery and hidden in underground caverns from generation to generation." She spread out the spotless clothes
as she continued, "Each of these has a special significance.
The wise among our people are familiar with their meaning. Also, they are aware of the coming birth of your son.
From the garments made of these, they will recognize him
as the one whom they seek."

She lifted and spread before Mary a cloth of white silk
embroidered in stripes of blue. "This indicates your child
is of royal birth."

Next, she raised a wide band of red silk. "This means
that he came from the land of Moab, through Ruth, the
Moabitess."

The third cloth was of many colors. Elizabeth held this
one in her hands for some time. Her voice grew husky
with reverence. "This one, of many colors, is worn by the
Prince of the House of David."

Mary was conscious of the firm, purposeful beat of her
heart. At once she was proud and humble.

"Jacob made Joseph a coat of many colors," Elizabeth
continued, holding the cloth close to her breast, her brightened eyes reflecting the magnificent happenings of the
past, "indicating his father chose him to be Prince, head of

his house, even though he was a younger son."

Gently, she refolded this cloth and lifted the fourth and last. It was white, with a wide border of embroidered plaid at the bottom. Elizabeth ran her fingers over the rich, heavy plaid and explained, "The gold in the plaid was sewn with a needle made of wire. This is the symbol of the Prince of the Shepherd Tribes of the House of David."

At the sight of the plaid and hearing the word shepherd, a warm glow began in Mary's left side and radiated through her entire being.

During the days that followed, they employed themselves busily sewing clothes for the two babes. The tiny garments prepared for Elizabeth's child were plainer and took less effort than those for Mary's babe. At times, this caused Mary discomfort and embarrassment. One day, when Mary insisted on sewing clothes for Elizabeth's child and neglecting certain significant embroideries needed for her own baby's garments, Elizabeth laid her sewing basket aside and spoke in a solemn voice. "These are the first of many tasks we will do together during the coming years. It would be wise to understand certain things in the beginning. Among these things is the necessity to remove the emotion of human pride. If you pretend this is not true and attempt to prove it in your actions, you will succeed in proving but one thing."

Elizabeth gazed long into Mary's eyes, as if to once and for all raise this question and then clearly and finally settle it. Mary knew she was expected to ask the question, and she did so. "What does it prove?"

"It proves you feel me capable of jealousy! And by pretending importance to my child's clothes, you spare me the provocation of this jealousy." The needle in Mary's hand trembled as the wisdom of Elizabeth's words revealed the hypocrisy of certain established amenities in humanity's social relationships. "We will succeed," Elizabeth continued, "in that which is before us, to the extent we transcend the entanglement of emotions."

Relaxing from her solemnity, she added gently, "Hold no fear for my feelings. I do not suffer the pangs of foolish maternal pride."

One day at twilight, Mary and Elizabeth strolled through the village to enjoy the coolness of the evening breezes. Majestic cypresses stirred slightly in a stately fashion. The cooling air made more pungent the fragrance of the gardens they passed.

As they approached the outskirts of the village, a growing sense of peace pervaded Mary's entire being. Her world became hushed, yet expectant. In the stillness, of the Judean eventide was born a sense of unity with all creation. She seemed to share the same life that reared the trees skyward and yet hugged the earth with the smallest of the plants. She felt as though the life and meaning of all trees, plants, and flowers coursed through her; that she was colored by them and they were affected by having flowed through her. Each giving to the other the finest of its nature.

She paused at a carefully tended bush, attracted by a single rosebud. Mary felt a close affinity between the hidden beauty swelling into being within the rose and the life swelling into being within her. She sensed the expectancy in the way it was pointed upward toward the morrow's sun. She felt its very effort, an eager reaching outward and

upward, to unfold and release its fragrance to a higher
selfless communion. Mary, too, became selfless, unconscious of her own identity. She was the rose and the rose
was she.

While still absorbed in this rapturous unity, she was
distracted by a movement in the garden. She turned and
saw a young man, horribly bent and twisted in body but
with regular features and bright, sensitive eyes. He shuffled jerkily and it was obvious that this grotesque gait was
the only manner in which he could walk.

The ecstasy of her union with the rose still filled her as
Mary gazed at the cripple. Suddenly, in her eyes, the body
of this young man was perfect and for his heart she saw
the eagerly unfolding rose....

A persistent tugging penetrated her consciousness. The
budding rose disappeared from her vision and she realized
the tugging was Elizabeth gently shaking her shoulder.
"Yes?" Mary asked confusedly.

Pale and solemn, Elizabeth nodded toward the young
man. His sensitive face frozen in astonishment, the young
man frantically felt of his perfectly formed torso, arms,
and legs. Finally convinced that his new body was real, he
fell at Mary's feet. "I know not who you are," he said, his
voice an awed whisper, "but this was done by you!"

With a glance at Elizabeth, he said, "But I know you!"
and he arose and fled.

The two women stared at his departing figure. When he
was no longer in sight, Mary turned to Elizabeth. She was
almost as bewildered as the young man and a vague
uneasiness was in her heart. "What did I do?"

"That we do not yet know," Elizabeth replied, a new conviction burning deeply in her eyes. She took Mary in her arms, then lovingly and gently guided her toward home.

By noon the next day, the miraculous healing of Bozrah, the young man, was known throughout Hebron. The outer court of Elizabeth's home rapidly filled with people curious for a glance at this stranger who possessed such potent powers of healing. It was known to all that Bozrah had been deformed since birth, so only one capable of miracles could have wrought this change in him.

Within the privacy of their chamber, Mary and Elizabeth sat silently together while the noise outside continued. As the tumult grew, a deep uneasiness troubled Mary. Her feelings were tinged with a vague, uninterpretable sense of guilt that she could neither define nor remove.

A servant entered discreetly, announcing that in the court were deformed people clamoring for Mary to perform more miracles. Even after the servant had gone, the silence between the two women continued. Mary knew her wise, older cousin well enough to know that this was one problem on which she would receive no advice. They both knew that in healing Bozrah, Mary had handled holy powers and in Elizabeth's face, Mary saw her intention to remain silent in the matter. It was not an indifferent or critical silence, but a reticence bespeaking love and sympathy that implied that in matters such as these, she was incapable of offering counsel.

In her heart Mary knew she, too, was incapable of knowing what she should do. There were those people in the court. Should she go out? And if she did, would she

see in them the same budding perfection she saw in
Bozrah? If she could, she had no doubt but they would be
healed of their deformities.

But something stopped her. Could it be because she
detected a tone of indignation in the servant's announcement that his master's house had been assailed by such
rabble? Mary felt that those who waited for a miracle in
the court did so in a spirit similar to the spectators who
occupy tiers in the amphitheater, impatiently awaiting the
sensationalism presently to be enacted for their entertainment.

Earnestly she searched within herself for a decision.
Her thoughts turned to the sun. It would help her. It
always had. Quickly, she left the room and hurried to the
roof. She looked for a long time into its brightness, hard
and impersonal at this time of day. Because her need was
so great and her desire so sincere, she pled fervently.

Finally, she was rewarded. The same voice! She could
never forget its gentle authority. She clung breathlessly to
every word. Her eyes flooded with tears of joyful humbleness. She listened intently so that she would not miss a
single word.

"This is the answer to that which concerns you so
deeply. No person suffers because of a neglectful God.
Human beings build their own body by their past and present thoughts and deeds. Creation contains no accident or
injustice. That which appears as physical misfortune is but
the love of God operating in a concealed manner, providing special experience needed by the deformed. When that
particular experience has served its purpose, the appearance of misfortune will be no more.

"Until this time is come, we must not remove the seeming handicap, lest we disturb the plans of God. God planted good in all and it is this plan that will unfold. If we first awaken the good in another, then we may remove the means that God uses in bringing forth the good. But if we remove the means before the end is accomplished, before the good is unfolded, then their purpose is defeated."

The voice stopped. Mary was breathless, wondering if there would be more. She became calm with a new poise and assurance. The voice would speak no more for she knew the answer to her question – only in one's heart can one's body be healed. For a person's body is but the manifestation of that which is lived in his or her heart.

She returned to the room and spoke to Elizabeth. "What I have unwittingly done is not good. I shall return home at once. When the crowds learn of my departure, they will leave you in peace."

Elizabeth's only reply was a sympathetic nod of her head.

At this moment, the servant re-entered. Excitedly, he related the news that was spreading about and that he thought his mistress should know. The story was that Bozrah had always coveted his brother's beautiful wife. So when he was made perfect, he tried to rob his brother of his wife. But the wife still preferred her husband.

Without comment, Mary and Elizabeth listened to the story. When it was over and the servant gone, Mary said aloud as though in echo to the words of the sun. "His heart had not been healed first!"

Elizabeth placed a comforting kiss upon Mary's forehead and left to supervise preparations for the journey to Nazareth.

CHAPTER 9

When the caravan of Mary and Joseph reached their home in Nazareth, members of their household raced joyfully out to welcome them. And Zaele, the independent and defiant, let the group. Zaele laughed and chattered with spontaneous vivacity apparently quite at ease now among the others. There was real interest expressed as she jumbled questions about the trip and her master and mistress with news of things that had been going on during their absence. Her spontaneity indicated that she was now happy in her present surroundings.

Mary was delighted with the change in Zaele and lost no time in arranging for an intimate talk. As soon as her household affairs were in order, Mary sent for her. Zaele's smile was humble and guileless as she came into Mary's presence. Holding forth her hand, Mary led her to a bench where they sat side-by-side.

"I am happy," Mary said affectionately, "that wounds of the past have left no scars."

Zaele's beautiful dark eyes glowed. Calmly she said, "The wounds were but to my pride. Their pain finally brought understanding to their purpose."

Mary was now convinced of the change in Zaele. "Seldom do we permit understanding to enter through any other door," she replied, then added, "Only through pain does the little lamb distinguish between the briar and the herb."

98

Zaele was alert with enlightenment.

Mary turned Zaele's palm up and patted it as one play-fully chastises a child. Then in a gentle tone she explained, "The more forceful our individuality and the more griev-ous our transgressions, the farther we travel in righteous-ness when once we find its true path."

Zaele's eyes filled with tears of gratitude. She crushed Mary's hand to her lips. In a voice broken with emotion, she said, "You are truly the wisest and most gracious of all women. Great is my debt for your mercy. Deep my shame for the manner in which I once accused you."

Mary rose and moved to the window to permit Zaele to conceal her tears. "Zaele," she said solemnly, gazing out across Nazareth's gently rolling hills, "you owe me noth-ing. We are like stones in a stream. The current rubs together our rough edges until our surface is smooth. Once our surface is smooth, there is no more friction. Is the smoothness of one stone indebted to the roughness of the other? Only because of the rough spots of each did the friction exist. Rough and smooth rub not together. If there be friction, there must be roughness on both stones.

"If you are in debt to me, then I, too, am in debt to you. For upon me was a roughness. It existed in the form of resentment. Resentment of the attitude of others toward me. In you, I personified all the attitudes and at you direct-ed all my resentment. The current of life rubbed you against me until my rough spot of resentment was made smooth."

Mary turned from the window. Zaele was now quiet, stilled with wonder at the words she had heard. Mary smiled companionably and said, "Now in our smoothness, we can move together without discord."

Zaele's stillness continued. Mary watched the facial evidence of a question forming in her mind. Zaele turned cleared eyes upon Mary and asked, "Would it not also be true that the smoothed stones no longer have need of each other?"

Mary thrilled at the completeness of Zaele's reasoning. "So very true!" she affirmed. "Far greater would they be needed by those who still rub their roughness together and know not why."

Zaele heaved a tremulous sigh of despair. Mary's heart gladdened as she interpreted the sigh. Casually, she asked, "Is it your wish to return to the temple?"

Zaele sprang to her feet. "Could I?" she whispered, her volatile energies suspended in mid-air.

Mary, so moved by the intensity of Zaele's desire, could answer only by nodding her head. When she could speak, she said, "Halhul is wise and good. He sent you the message that 'ignorance in the child can be traced to the fault of the father.'"

Mary moved from the window and, standing before Zaele, gazed deeply into her eyes. "Halhul would like to have you back." Then she added in prophetic tone, "Little does he realize that his need of you is now greater than yours of him."

With shining eyes, she drew herself erect. In a manner almost like a ceremonial command, she instructed, "Go prepare for a triumphal return to the home of your disgrace. Through humility you have earned honor. You shall re-enter the gates of the temple attended by a caravan. A caravan whose trappings will be those of the Royal House of David."

When Joseph returned from delivering Zaele to the temple, he brought back a letter from Elizabeth. At sight of it, Mary exclaimed hopefully, "It has happened! Her son is born!"

She reached eagerly for the scroll. Joseph turned to go. Mary touched his arm, staying him. "These things are not without the part you play. Never was a heart more generous or a hand more willing. Included are you in Elizabeth's thoughts and I would have you share with me the contents of her message."

Joseph's devotion to Mary flooded his face as he seated himself to listen. She broke the seal, unrolled the scroll, and in a low voice read:

Beloved, because of your anxiety for my welfare, I send you this message that our son is now born and all is well! For the first time since his birth, the house if finally at rest from the zealous stir of kindred and neighbors. And, as usual, the most active of all was cousin Zabez.

Mary lowered the scroll and, curbing her interest in what was to follow, declared with appreciation, "How like Elizabeth! Child-birth at her age must have been an arduous task. But little will we learn of it from her. Instead, she jests of cousin Zabez's officious presence." She shook her head in affectionate exasperation and resumed reading.

However, we are much in debt to cousin Zabez. If her determined interference had not so outraged Zacharias, he might not have regained his power of speech!

Mary and Joseph smiled happily into each other's eyes at the news of Zacharias' recovery.

It happened at the circumcision. Everyone affirmed the babe's name should be Zacharias. When I protested, say-

ing his name should be called John, you should have heard the confusion. Our kindred searched seven genera- tions back and found not a single John! In seeking to over- rule me, they appealed to Zacharias.

Zacharias asked for a writing table and wrote that the child was to be called John. Even though everyone mar- veled at this transgression of the custom, they accepted it. All but Zabez!

She defiantly handed the writing board back to Zacharias and demanded an explanation. Though the board trembled in her hands, her back was straight, held fast by the traditions of Judah. Zacharias' eyes blazed! He broke the writing tablet to bits and, turning on the crowd, announced in thundering, irrevocable tones that the name of the child was to be John!

Mary lowered the scroll and she and Joseph were silent as each savored the scene described by Elizabeth. Then again she read.

Zacharias moved to the crib and addressed the babe. As he did, the light of Holy Breath shone about him. These are the words he said:

"And you, child, shall be called the prophet of the King who will deliver us from the hand of our enemy; for you shall go before the arrival of the Lord to prepare the ways of His people. To prepare them to receive the knowledge of salvation from the highest, by teaching them to remove the crusts of their ignorance. To give light to them that sit in darkness and to guide our feet into the presence of this master of love."

These wondrous things Zacharias said, but since has hardly spoken. Though his speech is returned, my once proud, grandiloquent husband is now meek and silent. His only interest is in the welfare of John, who daily waxes stronger in body and spirit.

Yesterday, something happened that gives me concern. Two Roman soldiers brought a message from the temple summoning Zacharias to return at once. Why should Roman soldiers be messengers of the temple? Why, indeed, unless the temple has displeased the Palace. And why summons of Zacharias, unless he was the cause of the displeasure?

If his prophecy concerning little John has reached the ears of Roman royalty, then such action is explained. They would know more of this King of whom he spoke, who comes to deliver us from our enemy. With regret, I burden your hearts with this anxiety. I do so because it concerns you, also. We must recognize this warning and realize that our mutual path of purpose is fraught with many dangers!

Thus the letter was finished. They sat in heavy silence. Finally, a deep breath stirred the powerful frame of Joseph. Mary was still, lest he wanted to speak his feelings. He murmured as though to himself, "Poor Zacharias!"

Mary waited silently. Joseph's luminous eyes were fixed in the depths of abstraction, so deep was his concentration. His words were low and deliberate when he spoke. "Poor Zacharias, like so many of the Sadducees and Pharisees, is caught in a snare of his own construction. The Romans only tolerate them because of their control over the people.

"Does not the law, which compels a Jew to carry the burden of a Roman soldier for a mile, sufficiently show the Roman's contempt for the Jew. If the people were not

controlled by the synagogue and the temple, they would
have to be controlled by the Roman armies. This would
dig deeply into the purse of Augustus in Rome. So the
Pharisees and Sadducees are allowed to flourish!"

Joseph sighed and his tone grew bitter. "The Jews in
power use diverse means to control the people. Paraded
wisdom is one. The supposed wisdom of the priests and
scribes is revered by the people because to them it carries
the power to open the gates of Jehovah's blessings. The
man in the street is taught that this wisdom is attainable
only through the temple or the synagogue. The reason it is
unattainable is that the mysteries of the Sadducees are oral.
They can be communicated only from one priest to another. Because the secrets are so notoriously guarded, the people's imagination is excited – to the extent that fantastic
powers are attributed to this withheld knowledge."

Joseph's insight enlightened Mary. Now she understood
many things that had puzzled her when she lived in the
temple. The sincere, like Halhul, were subordinated by the
crafty, such as Ananias.

"The Pharisees have a *different* yet *similar* situation,"
Joseph continued. "They are exponents of the written law.
Consequently, their scrolls are available and can be read
by the people." Joseph's eyes burned deeper and a trace of
irony crept into his voice. "But loudly do they proclaim
that the power of the written law is concealed within its
interpretation. Consequently, its power and benefits belong
to none but the priests. For only they know the secret
chamber wherein is applied the proper interpretation of
this written law!"

A note of pity returned, softening the irony in his tone.
"Thus, the people's inadequacy is held before them. If

they are not priests, they cannot enter this chamber of interpretation. Therefore, they are deprived of God's good unless...."

Joseph paused. "Unless," he winced at the painfulness of his own words, "unless they go to the priests bearing gifts of worldly goods, in exchange for which the priests invoke special blessings for them from Jehovah. To prove their power, they establish a market place of death, their bloody altars where innocent life is bought and sold. As intended, this atrocity duly impresses the people. For they feel that only those favored by special intimacy with God would dare lay such flagrant hands upon creatures of God's creation."

Joseph was silent. Mary watched as his indignation subsided. When again he spoke, the resentment was gone, leaving only despair. "In claiming the right to administer the blessings of God, they deprive them from everyone, including themselves. With unholy hands, they handle unholy things. Unholy hands that they in turn hold up to the people as so righteous as to be beyond their reach!"

Joseph rose and strode up and down. "Poor Zacharias," he continued. "Long he manipulated the true wisdom of the law. We cannot handle the earth without soiling our hands. Neither can we expose ourselves to wisdom without awakening within us its counterpart. Zacharias has been sufficiently awakened to see the pecuniary premeditation underlying the temple's performance. A performance he participated in all his life. Now, he can see no way to break away, even thought to continue torments his soul.

"Probably, there are many among the priests and scribes who secretly writhe in the noose of a similar snare. For them there is no escape. If they appealed to the people, they would be stoned for deception. The Romans would interpret it as loss of control over the people and promptly deal with is as such.

"So," Joseph said with regretful finality, "Zacharias and all others who have grown truly wise feel the bite of the snare woven from the fibers of their own desire for wealth and honor." His eyes gazed directly into Mary's. Deep in his eyes, Mary saw anguished pity for Zacharias.

"Is there naught we can do for him?" she asked.

Joseph shook his head. "He could hide in the hills with our kindred, the Shepherds, if all he sought was to save his life. But if I know the heart of Zacharias, it is not his remaining years with which he is concerned, it is with his actions during the years he has already lived."

He shook his head resignedly. "No, there is naught we can do," he declared.

Then a confident lilt swelled in his voice. "But there is much Zacharias can do." With profound assurance, he added, "And much he will do!"

CHAPTER 10

A s the time for the birth of her son drew nearer, Mary felt a certain conviction grow stronger. The voice that had first announced to her that she had been chosen to have this child also said that the throne of David would be given unto him. Her conviction was that if he were to inherit David's throne that he should be born in Bethlehem, the City of David. For it was there that David was born and crowned King of the Shepherd Tribe and it was prophesied that the heir to his throne would also be born there.

As these thoughts became clearer as to their purpose, she began to understand why the inn in Bethlehem had held such a strangely magnetic attraction for her. She attempted to reason away the persistency of this feeling. Joseph had so busied himself and his household in preparation for the coming of her babe that she feared she would be unable to make him understand why she preferred to leave his home and the comforts he had prepared for her and make this painful journey to a crowded and uncomfortable inn – and there, among strangers and privations, undergo the ordeal of childbirth.

Also, even if he did understand her feelings, she knew it would be a sharp disappointment to him because she had detected in his attitude, as he directed the preparations, a pride and pleasure never before displayed.

This particular morning found her conflicting feelings

highly intensified. The time was now so close she must either forget Bethlehem or prepare immediately to make the journey. While she struggled for the true answer, Joseph entered. Mary was shocked by the force of his restrained emotion. Never had she seen his face so set or his eyes so blazing. When he spoke, she marveled at the quietness of his voice.

"I have just received an announcement from Cyrenius, Governor of Syria, that Caesar Augustus has decreed that all the world be taxed!"

Mary saw the crushed mass in his hand that must be the announcement. "What does it mean?" she questioned sympathetically.

"It means I must go to Bethlehem. It is there my taxes are to be paid!" came the answer in words of stone.

Mary's heart leaped. "When?" she asked, holding her breath.

She could see the struggle within him before he attempted to answer. "Now!" he declared, the heat of his rebellion at Caesar's tyranny escaping through his restraint. "Now!" he repeated, "when your need of me could be no greater, I must journey to Bethlehem to replenish the ever-empty coffers of Rome's treasury!"

Mary's scalp tingled at this evidence of a divine hand in her affairs. The decision had been made for her. She would go to Bethlehem with Joseph. Splendid Joseph! His concern and pride were so tensely focused upon her and her unborn child. She motioned for him to sit at her side.

Taking his knotted fist, she gently straightened his fingers, holding them closely and warmly until all tension was gone and their touch became as tender with care as were her own. Then in soothing tones she spoke. "I know how deep is your concern. But deeper than our feelings and plans runs a greater purpose. A purpose so powerful that even circumstances move with its will. Since first I saw the birthplace of David it has seemed unnatural that the heir to his throne should be born anywhere save in the self-same place."

Mary could feel Joseph grow tense again. His objections came quickly. "The motion of the camel would be beyond your endurance. Both you and the child might be injured. Time has wrought great change in the house of David's birth. It is now a common inn."

Mary felt his clasp tighten with anxiety as he hopefully suggested, "Could it not be that you misinterpreted this feeling for the inn? Nothing is now there of the glory that was David's."

Mary gently unflexed his fingers as she replied. "Listen closely and I will tell you where still the glory lies. It lives in the heart of every shepherd who hungers for his own Shepherd by whom he can be comforted as surely and completely as his sheep are comforted by him. Because of this hunger, their hope is ever turned toward Bethlehem, the City of David from whence, according to the prophets, shall come this Holy Shepherd. Is it not fitting that this one they seek should be born where he is sought?"

For a long time Joseph was silent in thought. When again he spoke, his voice was fresh and vibrant with new conviction. "May I never again question the purpose of your wishes!" Then with voice lowered in reverence, he added, "And may I ever be allowed to serve in their fulfillment."

On their way to Bethlehem, they had to pass through

the narrow streets of Jerusalem, now crowded with the
masses of milling men and beasts answering Rome's
decree that all the world be taxed. Even the progress of a
caravan bearing the trappings of the House of David could
be measured by the span of a man's hand. His anxious
face as white as his headdress, Joseph skillfully edged
their caravan through the surging mass.

After long and seemingly futile effort, Herod's Gate
was reached and they emerged beyond the city's walls.
Free at last from the weary tug and thrust of traffic, Joseph
rested his caravan. With gentle hands, he lifted Mary from
her camel and carried her to a place of comfort prepared
beneath an olive tree. Upon his knees, he deftly arranged
cushions and robes and then, rising to his feet, stared in
helpless anxiety upon the placid face of his beloved.

Smiling into his drawn face, she said, "Poor Joseph,
would that you might worry less. No woman ever lived
who would not gladly take my place this day. With each
pain comes joy beyond belief." She reached up and took
his hand, urging softly, "Lie beside me and have the rest
you need."

Dazedly, Joseph obeyed. Mary sat erect, her back
against the cushioned tree, her face tranquil and shining.
Tirelessly, she stroked Joseph's head at her side until his
concern for her dropped away and he slept. At that
moment, she was the universal mother of all humankind.
Within the protective wall of her womb was infant man,
vigorously reacting to nature's impulse to be born into a
mother's care. While at her side, protected by the affectionate vigilance of the same motherly care, slept Joseph,
man at his maturity.

Not until a procession crossed the highway and passed

near the trees where his caravan rested did Joseph stir from his sleep. When he realized he had slept while Mary sat erect stroking his head when instead she should have rested, he rose in quick shame. Smiling an unfathomable smile, Mary quieted his unuttered contrition and caused him to resume his place beside her.

The procession interested her. It consisted of men, women, and children. Among them were shepherds and each bore in his arms three lambs. Many of the women and children carried evergreen wreaths and some had young evergreen trees. They all carried something in their hands or arms and were quick of motion, happy in spirit, and light of heart. This happy spontaneity, in such contrast to the dogged dejection within the city's walls, refreshed Mary and the nature of the objects they carried fascinated her.

Without taking her eyes from the procession, she pressed Joseph's hand for attention. "What is the manner of this procession? The words of their song escape me."

After watching them a moment, Joseph answered. "It is a customary ritual of the common people. They sing because a child has been born to one of them." His gaze shifted ahead in the direction they were going. "See that cluster of poor houses and stables?" he pointed.

Following his direction, Mary nodded. "They are going there," he explained, "because to parents living in one of those meager shelters a child has been born in a stable. The words of the song you hear are 'A child is born to us in the stable!' This means the child is of the people and, as one of them, will be another friend and benefactor. To the people, this is a very important and significant occurrence."

"Those things the people carry, what do they mean?"

"They are gifts," Joseph answered. "Everyone presents a gift, even the children. No babe born in the stable remains poor. The women give of their jewels, the men of their goods and spices, and the shepherds of their lambs."

"Why the wreaths and young evergreen trees?" Mary question.

"Evergreens retain their life even though the changing seasons when the finger of death is upon the leaves and flowers of other plants. These green trees and wreaths are symbols that the life of humankind is also retained through the changing states of birth and death.

"Though the people are as numerous as leaves upon the trees, they are helpless and alone. Enemies surround them and foes dwell among them. They are intimidated by the cruel rattle of Roman armor and exploited by the greedy swish of priestly robes. But the enemy dwelling among them is the greatest – their ignorance."

To Mary everything became clear. Now she knew why David's birthplace had tugged so insistently at her heart. All the parts fit together. When she spoke, it was not only to Joseph, but to all creation. "Where should the one who is to overcome their enemies be born?" Her words were vibrant with purpose. "In the luxury of the palace? Amid the grandeur of the temple? Amidst the wealth of the House of David?"

She paused. In her eyes shone a heavenly light. "Or should he be born in a stable manger so the people know he is also one of them!"

Mary continued, "The true heritage of the Throne of David is the love of the people. The kingdom of his psalms will live long after his buildings crumble and the boundaries of his lands are forgotten. It is fitting that the heir to the throne of David be born in Bethlehem, the City of David. But it is also fitting that the redeemer of the people be born in a stable. Therefore, we will go to the City of David and find a stable that the savior of the people may be found in a manger."

Joseph did not speak and Mary felt his silence was more indulgence to her mood than acceptance of her words.

Bethlehem was also crowded with people come to be taxed. But much more readily than in Jerusalem was a caravan of the House of David given the right of way. The instant the symbol of its trappings was recognized, a way was automatically cleared for its progress.

Not until the inn was reached did Joseph stop. Quickly dismounting, he hurried to the side of Mary's camel. He did not look up at her as he said, "In our agreement with those who operate the inn it was stipulated that a certain room be at all times held available against the possibility of our need."

Mary stared at the milling crowd. Quite obvious was the logic of the words of Joseph as they welled up from his anxious heart. Her love of him rebelled at the necessity of ignoring his deep concern for her. In her perplexity, she glanced at the door of the inn. Roman soldiers moved back and forth through its opening in a constant activity of haughty officiousness. The feeling suddenly swept over her that the responsibility of deciding where her child should be born was no longer her responsibility.

She said to Joseph, "It is certainly the right of an honorable man to provide comfort for his wife when it is her time. Pray forgive my interference and go do as you would about this thing."

Relief raised his head and brightened his face. With purposeful strides, he moved to the door and wedged himself through with the stream of entering soldiers.

Mary busied her attention with the harried dejection of the people in the street. There was an abrupt disturbance at the door of the inn. The entering soldiers were momentarily congested by the forthright exit of a large man. At first Mary did not recognize the man as Joseph. As he moved toward her, she saw his effort to remove from his face the evidence of his feelings.

When he spoke, his voice was warped and strained. "There is no room in the inn. Every room is occupied by Roman soldiers. Even the manager has been removed from his quarters!"

Mary's heart sang. Now she knew why she had felt the responsibility of the decision had been taken out of her hands. She reached down and warmly clasped Joseph's shoulder as she said, "Again the curve of circumstance has pointed the way. Fret not and observe how clearly our actions are directed in accordance with a purpose that transcends my comfort and your personal honor and even extends to Rome and back. The soldiers who occupy our room in the inn are but additional pawns in this great purpose."

She paused and affectionately watched the struggle in Joseph as, ceasing to be a husband, he became an obedient and enthusiastic assistant. "Again, you must forgive me," he said. "You need but name your wishes. I may not comprehend their meaning, but I will not doubt the divinity of their purpose!"

A wondrous light radiated her face as she said, "Go put at rest your caravan. Then find the most humble of the beasts of burden. Upon it I would ride, and with you walking at my side, we will go in search of that which waits for us."

CHAPTER 11

In the outer fringe of Bethlehem, Joseph found a large, unoccupied cave. Customarily, the cave was used as a shelter for beasts of burden. Inside was a manger, a bench, and fresh straw upon its earthen floor. "Here it shall be!" Mary announced softly through lips white with pain.

Tenderly, Joseph lifted her from the donkey and in his arms carried her inside. There, upon a couch made from his robes, he gently laid her. Then he stood erect, helpless, and frantic.

Mary's paled lips smiled with appreciation as she looked up into his face distorted with anxiety. "Go, now," she instructed affectionately, "and the first woman you meet, ask of her if she will assist your wife in bring forth a child."

Joseph hesitated. His love for Mary cried out that she should have the best of cared administered by closest friends. And now, according to her words, he must fetch a stranger, probably a careless and unskilled stranger.

Mary spoke again. "Pray go at once. And remember it is to be the first woman you meet!"

Joseph hesitated no longer, but stumbled out of the cave, striding rapidly toward the center of Bethlehem. He was almost blind with fear and his heart thumped painfully with the possibility that he was neglecting his husbandly responsibility in obeying Mary's wishes.

He passed an old shepherd perched upon a rock, his small frame huddled over his staff. The shepherd hailed him with a salutation. Joseph automatically and impatiently returned the salutation without breaking his stride. Then after a few steps, he stopped in his tracks, turned and stared incredulously toward the little shepherd. The shepherd was a shepherdess, a little old woman with face wrinkled and dried by the sun and time, but in her eyes shone the clarity of timelessness.

Joseph slowly retraced his steps until he stood before her. The placid clearness of her face made him feel as awkward and inexperienced as a child. Quickly, he asked of her that which Mary had instructed him. She pursed her withered lips and emitted a shrill, significant whistle. Instantly, a huge shepherd dog was at her side. With unexpected agility, she descended from the rock and signaled to the dog. The dog leaped upon the rock, seated himself, and instantly assumed vigilance over her small herd.

"Now, Joseph, son of David," said the little shepherdess, "I am ready to return the kindness you bestowed on me at the Damascus Gate in Jerusalem."

With astonishment, Joseph recognized her as the little shepherdess whom he had protected from the men making way for the merchant's caravan the day Mary left the Temple.

With no further word, the woman led off in the direction of the cave. Following at her heels, Joseph marveled at her speed and at the strange turn of events. She went directly toward the cave where Mary waited, without the necessity of being so guided, and Joseph marveled still more. He could not put from him the feeling but that she had been waiting for his arrival. However, his confidence in her so relieved his anxiety for Mary's welfare that all other things seem unimportant.

Not until they reached the cave did she stop. Just before entering, she turned and spoke. "I am Dalmatia. For a while, you will not be needed. North of where you found me, in an acacia grove, is my home. Go there to rest. Arestas, my grandson, will minister to your comfort."

Without waiting for his reply, Dalmatia prepared to enter the cave. But again she stopped and turned toward Joseph. With voice calm and assured, she added, "And as you rest, rest in peace."

Obediently, Joseph turned toward the spot where first he had seen Dalmatia. His acute fear for Mary's welfare had lifted as a black cloud suddenly blown away from the sun. He could think clearly again. Looking down at his sandal clad feet shuffling through the dust, he stopped. "Are you the feet of a child, dismissed by the wave of an old woman's hand?" he asked accusingly.

"Or are you the bearers of one who has reached the age of maturity? And as such," he added with a ring in his voice, "need not the counsel of women to determine your activity!"

Throwing back his splendid head, he stepped forward. This time his tread was measured and purposeful. "Rest indeed!" he exclaimed with ironical scorn to the wind whipping his cheeks. "There is man's work to be done in Bethlehem! So there we shall go!"

In Bethlehem, Joseph entered the crowded tax house. There a detestable *telonai* called for the properties and their respective taxes. If their owner was not present to answer and pay, the tax was heavily increased by a penalty.

Joseph recognized the *telonai* collecting the tax as the same one who had once in a trade attempted to rob him of his most valuable camel. Joseph wondered how many of his properties had already been called and penalized to deliberately swell the *telonai's* personal profits.

His name was spoken by one in the crowd. Turning, he saw two of his distant cousins. They, too, through far removed, were descendants of the House of David and as such owned considerable land and property in this district. As they made their way toward Joseph, he could not help but smile at their futile efforts to maintain an aloofness they felt due their wealth in the midst of the surging, unimpressed crowd that threatened to trample them underfoot.

With heavy indignation, they informed him that the tax collector, knowing that Joseph was absent, had already called and penalized much of his property. They were momentarily abashed when their important information brought from Joseph nothing more than an unimpressed shrug of his shoulders. But they quickly recovered their poise. It was not theirs to understand this illustrious cousin, but to please him. With proper display of interest, one inquired for Mary's health.

Bluntly, Joseph replied, "At this very hour she brings forth a child!"

"It is unfortunate you must be so far from her!"

"She is here in Bethlehem," was Joseph's casual answer as he strained to hear the descriptions read by the tax collector.

The two cousins looked at each other with significant disbelief. Then one said with self-justified indignation," It would have been our wish that one of our homes be placed at the disposal of our kin at such a time. Pray, with whom does she abide?"

Joseph answered without removing his attention from the *telonai*. "She is in a stable near here with an old shepherdess." Momentarily, he turned his gaze from the tax collector and let it rest upon his cousins, then with finality declared. "It is she who is to have the babe. It was her wish that it occur in a stable!" As though this closed the subject, he returned his attention to the activities of the tax collector.

The two cousins glared at each other with as much indignation as they dared. One gathered courage enough to suggest with a tinge of scorn. "Is the babe's father without authority?"

Joseph's eyes lost their sharp awareness of his surroundings and in a voice free of feeling, he declared solemnly, "I am not the father of the child, neither is any other man!"

This time as the cousins looked at each other, it was with obvious uncertainty. Simultaneously, they motioned to each other to come outside where these incredulous statements could be properly considered.

Joseph was either unaware of heeded not their departure. At this moment, his name was called incoherently by the collector. Raising his hand and voice, he pushed majestically through the crowd and stood before the collection table. With eyes ablaze, he accused the oily *telonai*.

"Even after I was present, you attempted to describe my properties in a manner that I would not recognize them. You will now describe the property, collect the tax, and record its collection in the book of all my possessions in the province of Bethlehem. And neither you nor I shall move from where we stand until it is done!"

When Joseph left the tax house, he found his two cousins awaiting him. They had decided to overlook that which they should have condemned for fear of having failed to correctly hear Joseph's words. Also, even if they had heard him aright, it was very impractical to court the disfavor of their powerful cousin. Fawning in the proper manner, they expressed their desire to pay honor to Mary and the babe by their presence. Joseph led the way.

While they were yet quite a distance from the cave, they encountered many people coming and going. Reaching a little summit, Joseph paused and stared into the little valley he had left but a few hours earlier. Where before there had not been a person or a sound, there were now scores of people. Joyous people were singing and shouting at one another. And all the while, more people hurried past them toward the cave. Each person who passed bore a gift and wore a look of hopeful eagerness.

As Joseph and his cousins drew near, the shouts and songs became more distinct. The people's joy was unrestrained. Freely it moved from one to another with increasing buoyancy. Joseph stopped again and now stood transfixed. In the depths of his heart was an exquisite sensation as the words of the songs the happy people sang reached his ears.

> *The Prince of the House of David is born!*
> *Born to us in the stable!*
> *He is a ruddy child, fresh from the sun*
> *And straight from the hand of God!*
> *Our King, promised of the prophets*
> *Is surely come!*

Trailing dazedly, the two cousins followed as Joseph made his way to the door of the stable. Mary reclined upon a cushioned bench. In the manger lay the babe. Joseph looked for a sign of pain or fatigue, but try as he might, he could not see the details of her features. At first, he thought his eyes were blurred or had failed him. Then he detected a light around Mary's head and face. The light in itself was almost invisible, yet it prevented him seeing her features clearly and conveyed to him the certainty that hidden within this light were divine hands that gently and lovingly ministered to her.

Taking his place in the procession of people moving in and out, he approached the manger. In it he saw the babe. And he saw that the babe was also held in the arms and against the breast of this same light.

The swaddling clothes were arranged about the babe like petals of a rose, each cloth so arranged that its embroidery of age-old patterns and designs told their story to all who could read their meaning. White silk embroidered in stripes of blue bespoke his royalty. The garment of red silk meant that he came from the land of Moab through Ruth, the Moabitess. And the Cloth of Many Colors, as was the coat of Joseph, announced that here lay a Prince of the House of David.

As Joseph moved with the procession, he was just as deeply impressed as those jostling him from behind and holding him back from in front. As he neared the exit of the cave, he managed another glance at Mary. She was looking in his direction and motioned him to come to her. This time he could clearly see her features and never had he beheld a more glorious sight. It was difficult to look into the brilliance of her eyes. It was a brilliance not of the mid-day sun, but the glowing brightness of unfathomable joy.

She touched his hand and he felt as though his flesh would never be the same. "I would like Elizabeth to know," she said simply.

"A messenger shall leave at once," Joseph answered eagerly.

She turned her gaze to the manger as the alertly attentive Dalmatia re-arranged the babe's swaddling clothes. "Is not our child beautiful!" Mary breathed in a low voice.

Joseph's face instantly flashed a question. "Our child?" he echoed confusedly.

Mary slowly nodded. "Henceforth, he shall be our child." was the significant answer. Her gaze moved from the manger to the passing procession of people. Each showed awe or joy, according to their quality of feelings. Some wept, some laughed, some sang and chanted, while others simply stared in breathless silence at that which their eyes had long yearned to see.

"And," Mary continued, her voice but a whisper, "He belongs also to them. It was because of them he was born."

She turned back to Joseph and smiled the smile he knew was for him alone. She pressed his hand and spoke in a low voice. Joseph's heart sang at the return of their intimacy. "Dalmatia has asked that we bide a while with her. Pray have the presents removed to her home. From there, they may be redistributed to the poor." She smiled the sweetest of companionable smiles and closed her eyes to rest.

On leaving the cave to perform Mary's wishes, Joseph

was delighted to see his friend, Arioch, and two other
shepherds in the procession that now extended as far as he
could see. Arioch was the devout and upright leader of the
Shepherd Tribe. Years had passed since Joseph had last
seen his esteemed friend and he affectionately clasped his
arms.

Arioch's greeting was abstracted and impersonal, as a
man still in a dream he is loathe to relinquish. Joseph was
hurt. Dropping his hands, he stared with uncertainty and
turned to go. Arioch stopped him, placing a hand on his
shoulders. As Arioch's struggle with his abstraction
became obvious, Joseph knew something unusual had happened to his old friend and was ashamed of his first reaction toward him.

When Arioch did speak, his words seemed strange to
the people gathered around, but not to Joseph. Arioch told
how, in the fields to the south, while he and the other two
shepherds were keeping watch over their flocks, a great
glory had shone around them so dazzling that their eyes
had been blinded and they had become sore afraid.

While yet they could not see, they had heard a voice
that said unto them, "Fear not, for behold I bring you good
tidings of great joy which shall be to all people. For unto
you is born this day in the City of David, a Savior, who is
Christ the Lord."

As Arioch repeated in calm ringing tones the words he
had heard from heaven, the crowd increased around him.
People approached on quieted feet, with intent eyes and
straining ears to catch the strange words of this respected
shepherd. "You shall find the babe lying in a manger and
upon its swaddling clothes shall be a sign unto you."

Joseph could sense Arioch's abstraction returning as he

continued to recount that which the angel had said. "Goodwill toward one another sleeps within all humankind. He who is born to you this day shall begin its awakening. Thus stirring toward fruition the day when there will be peace on earth to all people of good will!"

Arioch's countenance became clear. With pleased recognition, he looked into the sea of rapt faces. In a low-pitched voice that imparted a sacred impressiveness to each thought, he said, "As if, for ere, the earth had awaited the arrival of this moment, it lifted forth its voice in praise of God, its song ringing from hill and vale. And it seemed that the hosts of heaven came down, blending their voices with this song of the earth. As thought the forces of heaven and earth harmonized in the mutual purpose of achieving that of which they sang. 'From humankind's goodwill toward one another, shall come peace on earth.'"

Arioch lowered his noble head in grateful humility. Then turning his face toward the cave, patiently he took his place in the procession that he might now see him of whom he had heard the angels sing. And as Joseph made his way through the crowd toward the home of Dalmatia, the beat of his heart shook his frame and his eyes were blinded with tears from the wonder of that which had been revealed to Arioch.

When Joseph brought Mary and Jesus to Dalmatia's home, he thought the constant stream of worshipers would subside. But instead, it increased. It was as though all Judea had been waiting to make this pilgrimage.

Two contrasting processions from opposite directions moved slowly up the gently sloping valley of the acacia grove. Both met at Dalmatia's neat little home in the shade of the trees heavy with their yellow blossoms. One column

was composed of those who bore gifts for the holy child
and the other column was made up of diseased and
deformed beggars.

Customarily, the presents given by the people to an
infant born in a stable were retained by the babe's parents
so that one born to the people would not remain poor.
Though born in a stable, Jesus was the wealthiest prince of
Palestine, heir to the House of David, and even holder of
the title to the land upon which stood entire cities.
Therefore, he needed not presents from those who could
give. But those who could, needed to give. And those who
could not, needed to receive.

Those who brought gifts entered one door, placed their
presents around the babe's crib and received the blessing
of Mary's smile. When there was room for no more presents, this door was closed and another opened, through
which came the ragged, the diseased and deformed. With
reverent orderliness, they selected for themselves one of
the many gifts. Then as they departed, they became
unaware of the prize tightly hugged to their vacant breast,
so dazed were they by the radiance of Mary's smile. Thus,
did both the giver and the receiver carry away with them
another greater gift.

Looking out a window, Joseph saw a caravan approaching in between the two processions. The splendid camels
were richly accoutered, obviously bearing wealthy and
honored travelers. As Joseph watched the caravan, he was
impressed that all levels of persons, though coming from
different directions, met at the same place. The three processions, the people, the people's poor, and the people's
rich, were all part of the same pilgrimage as result of the
same hope.

When Joseph recognized the swaying dignity of
Zacharias at the head of the caravan, he rushed out to meet
them. Among the acacia trees near the house he waited.
The camel behind Zacharias carried a sheltered litter and
soon Joseph could make out the form of Elizabeth holding
what must be John, her half-year-old son.

Not until Zacharias had dismounted from his kneeling
camel did Joseph step out from the trees to greet him.
With a cry of joy, Zacharias rushed forward to greet him.
Together, they assisted Elizabeth and John to dismount.
Elizabeth's greeting to Joseph was a radiant face and a significant squeeze of his arm as he and Zacharias lifted her
from the litter.

Joseph led them into the presence of Mary and the
babe, then departed. From upon their knees, with beggar
and thief at their side, this elderly and illustrious couple
and the infant John paid honor to Mary and Jesus.

Zacharias, the first to rise, moved nearer to Mary. He
struggled with words to express the fullness of his heart.
Mary, seeing his difficulty, spoke for him. "Now that you
three are here, all is complete. I feel Joseph's impatience
as he waits outside for his friend. And there is naught here
for which you are needed." Zacharias feasted his eyes
again upon the swaddled figure of Jesus and then departed
to rejoin the waiting Joseph.

Elizabeth raised her bowed head and faced Mary. As
their eyes met, the room was aglow with light, a soft,
golden light. Yet so unbearable to some was its brilliance
that they fled from the room. Those who remained seemed
not affected. But one needed but to look into their faces to
see the pureness of their hearts.

Beside the crib of Mary's babe was a waiting empty

crib. Glancing toward it, Mary smiled and her joy made
her smile so brilliant that none but Elizabeth could see her
face. "Lay John beside Jesus," she said, "and come and
watch with me."

CHAPTER 12

It was eventide, the first watch, and caught in the unreal veil of twilight was all creation. Fires were being lit throughout the wooded slopes leading to Dalmatia's house, around which grouped those who must wait for the morrow to see the long-awaited Messiah. On the porch, among comfortable rugs, sat Mary and Elizabeth with their infants in their arms. Joseph and Zacharias sprawled in the grass nearby while Dalmatia, ever silent, gracious, and removed, sat on her heels, shepherd fashion, at the far end of the porch.

The evening breeze wafted up to the house the sounds from the grove: bits of songs, joyous greetings, voices animated in excited conversation, the congenial clatter of metal vessels as some cooked a sparse evening meal. The gathering dusk accentuated the contrast of fires and shadowy trees while the movement among them of figures robed in brilliant colors cast a spell as though some magnificently portentous ceremony was being enacted.

Then through the grove moved a sudden stillness. As the silence became more acute, Joseph and Zacharias got to their feet, their eyes searching the flickering fires and shadows for its cause. Finally, they saw why. The people had lined up on both sides of the trail to watch three white-clad men riding three of the largest camels ever to be seen in Palestine.

The rider on the first camel, though he rode with the

rhythm of youth, was obviously thrice older than
Zacharias. Behind him rode a tremendous man, his broad
shoulders rolling above the heads of the others, his skin
black and gleaming like priceless ebony beneath the
whiteness of his diadem. The third rider was a youth.

The old one halted the caravan. In deference to his
independence of action, the other two remained upon their
beasts until he had dismounted. From the stilled spectators
came a sudden cry of incredulous joy. Joseph, the dignified, deliberate monarch among men, swept with spontaneity, rushed forward as a child running toward the
unexpected arrival of a beloved father.

"Gaspar! Gaspar!" he cried, over and over. The old one
opened his arms and Joseph rushed into their embrace.

Releasing Joseph, the venerable Gaspar spoke, his
voice calm and mild. "It is a glorious time, my son." He
turned to the other two. "Joseph," he announced, indicating the huge, dark man, "This is Balthasar, who comes
from the lands south of Egypt." Then he nodded to the
younger man. "This is Melchior of Parthia. We three, with
others from different lands, were gathered together, seeking guidance in the course of nations, peoples, tribes, and
tongues. Near the banks of the Euphrates, we sat in silent
communion. Those among us who could read the language
of the stars saw that he who would advance the coming
age had been born. We three were sent to follow his star
that we might do honor to him who is to be master of the
coming age!"

Joseph led the way to where Mary sat with Jesus on the
porch. The three sages of other lands placed their gifts
beside Mary and Jesus, then knelt upon the earth in silent
reverence. The gifts were nobility, symbolized by gold;

dominion and power, symbolized by myrrh; and divine wisdom, whose symbol is frankincense.

The infant Jesus stared with bright attentiveness at the impressive white figures. The ruddiness of his skin, the gold of his hair, and the glow of his eyes were as a lamp in the growing darkness.

Jesus and John were asleep in their cribs. Mary and Elizabeth stood at the window watching and listening to the council of men outside. Around a blazing fire sat the five. The flickering flames highlighted their strong, self-less faces, stilled by the seriousness of their responsibility.

Elizabeth's hand found Mary's as Gaspar portentous words reached their ears. He was relating to Joseph and Zacharias that which had happened in Jerusalem. Upon arriving there, the three wise men had inquired of many people where the newborn babe who was to become king of the age could be found. No one seemed to know. Herod, when he heard of their questioning, had summoned them to his court.

Gaspar explained, "There again, we had asked where the newborn king could be found, explaining that while yet beyond the Euphrates, we had seen his star rise and had come to pay him homage. Attempting to hide his fear, Herod called in council all the masters of Jewish law, demanding of them what the prophets had said concerning such a king.

"The Jewish masters answered with the words that the prophet Micah had written. 'Oh, Bethlehem Judea, a little place among the Judean hills, yet out of you will one come forth to rule over the tribes of Israel.'

"Also, other prophets had foretold that out of

Bethlehem would come the Messiah, the king who would rule over the tribes of Israel.

"After the Jewish masters were dismissed, Herod instructed us to continue to Bethlehem in search of such a king. And if we found the child, to return and tell him so that, he, too, could go and honor him."

Gaspar became silent. The fire burned low. No one spoke. Gaspar stirred himself. Rising, he kicked the fire alive, feeding it more roots. A cloud of sparks floated up to the starlit sky. Nearby, a disturbed thrush murmured anxiously. All eyes were fixed on Gaspar as he watched the sparks disappearing heavenward. He sighed as though weary with the load of man's malicious selfishness.

"Herod," he declared without shifting his stare from the heavens, "would destroy the babe! We shall return not by way of Jerusalem, but across the Syrian desert." He lowered his head and leveled his attention on the circle of gleaming, intent faces. His eyes blazed so that the fire seemed to pale.

The clasp of Mary and Elizabeth's hands tightened as with breathless fascination they drank in the significant spectacle taking place outside their window.

"Those who await our return," Gaspar stated, "Come from every race and clime. All are one in the human family and are anxious for tidings concerning this babe, who in the coming age shall mean so much to all."

Gaspar addressed his next words directly to Joseph and Zacharias. "These men stand ready to give of their wisdom and receive the wisdom that is to be his, their only concern being the enlightenment of all humanity. From this Jesus they will receive much. And much will they contribute to his awakening as to who he really is!" He looked sharply at Joseph. "Joseph, my beloved pupil, protection against the dangers of his generation until he reaches puberty is charged to you. At puberty, we will send for him. With our wisdom, we will awaken his divinity. Then he shall teach us. As the Christ, he will return here to his people!"

Moving over to Joseph and by the light of the fire, he drew a map on the ground and explained, "Near the second stream of the Nile where it empties into the sea and south of the ancient city of Zoan, is the home of Aziel and his wife, Phoebe. They will provide for your safety, comfort, and wisdom."

Standing with arms folded and head back, he stared into the ethers beneath the stars. Suddenly, as though he saw that for which he sought, he dropped his arms and announced with finality to Joseph. "You will begin the journey tonight. Herod sleeps not, and with the dawn will send his guards to kill the newborn king we came to honor."

By mid-morning of the following day, Mary, Jesus, and Joseph, with Elizabeth, John, and Zacharias, had reached Hebron, home of Elizabeth and Zacharias. Hebron was south of Bethlehem and on the road to Egypt.

The entire household soberly and hurriedly prepared what would be needed by Mary, Joseph, and Jesus on their journey to Egypt. Soon everything was ready. The members of the household, having received expressions of gratitude from Mary and Joseph, withdrew into the house. The two women, whose love for each other was so deep and sweet, gazed silently into each other's faces while they held their infants.

Joseph and Zacharias pretended to keep busy, tying and

untying harness pieces. Simultaneously, their pretense ceased and they lifted themselves to the fullness of their majestic heights, faced each other, and openly approached the significance of this farewell.

Joseph was the first to speak. "Would it not be best for all of you to come with us? Herod might spend his wrath on John!"

Zacharias glanced at Elizabeth, leaving to her the answer. With calm assurance, Elizabeth answered the silent inquiry of her husband. "I have no fear for the life of John. Neither Herod's wrath not plot of any man shall harm him while that for which he comes is yet undone. Willingly, I would go or stay. The decision I leave with my husband."

A whimsical smile lit the old patriarch's face. More to Joseph than to the others he answered, "We will not flee. The faith of Elizabeth will care for John. I am still a temple priest and, as such, must conduct ceremonies for the people. Henceforth, the nature of my work may prove strangely enlightening to the people, but to the Sanhedrin, it will prove quite disturbing."

He moved to where beautiful young Mary stood with Jesus in her arms. Holding her face between his hands, he placed his lips to her forehead. Then gently, he removed the protective cloth and stared into the luminous face of the sleeping Jesus. Deftly, reverently, tenderly, he replaced the cloth and without a word or backward glance hurried toward his house.

Joseph watched the figure of Zacharias until it disappeared, the he turned to Elizabeth. "Would that I possessed such strength and courage!" Moving close to Elizabeth, he looked down at John, who now being several months of age, was uncovered. Then Joseph lifted his gaze. Raising his eyes to Elizabeth's face, he gave her arm an affectionate clasp of encouragement and, without speaking, moved to the other side of the waiting caravan, leaving the two women alone.

For a time, they silently looked first at each other and then at each other's child. Finally, Mary broke the silence. With a gesture toward John, she asked, "May I?"

Elizabeth smiled the smile of the gods. Mary took John. Elizabeth took Jesus. Both women bowed their heads over the warm, living flesh held so closely to their breasts. Tears of humble gratitude filled their eyes. At this moment, the four of them were one.

When they re-exchanged their babes, little John was more alert to his surroundings than ever before. His large, dark eyes fastened anxiously upon the bundle that was Jesus. With one more glance at Elizabeth, Mary turned and walked toward the waiting caravan and Joseph. John began to squirm and whimper. With a chubby hand, he pointed toward the departing Mary and Jesus.

As the caravan moved away, Mary carried in her ears the cries of John; the heartbroken cry of an infant voicing its resentment against a loss it did not understand, but nevertheless a loss that was keenly felt.

A strange, fearful ache gripped Mary's heart as she realized that never before had either babe been heard to cry. Holding Jesus closer, she stared anxiously to the south, wondering about this unknown land and its strange people, a people among whom she must begin the responsibility of guiding toward maturity the holy infant at her breast.

CHAPTER 13

After many weary days, Mary, Joseph, and Jesus arrived at the ancient Egyptian city of Zoan. Upon the north-east end of the Nile Delta, beneath a deep blue sky, it rested from ageless activity, activity dating back as far as humanity had recorded. Under its Greek name, Tanis, kings of the sixth dynasty built a great temple. Rameses II chose the city as his residence and adorned it with many beautiful buildings.

Near the ruins of Rameses' Temple, surrounded by sunt and tamarisk trees, they found a small, listless bazaar. When Joseph inquired the way to the home of Aziel, the listlessness momentarily gave way to demonstrations of respect. It was obviously a great honor to go to the home of Aziel.

Buying aromatic melons from the way-shower, they continued their journey. It led through bright green fields scalloped with bare yellow rocks. Orchards were every-where. Trees of the orange, lemon, date, fig, apricot, olive, and locust were always in view for the Nile and its tribu-taries overflowed at regular intervals, maintaining the fer-tility of the delta.

Soon they approached higher ground. Upon a plateau was a large, aged sycamore grove. The warmth of the sun made pungent its spicy aroma. In the midst of the grove, surrounded by a well-kept clearing, they found a large rus-tic house. Like the trees, it was old and mellow. When they reached the clearing, two figures came from the house. Small and slender figures in simple garb; a man and a woman, with deep, bright eyes and gentle mien; ageless, mellow, and friendly. The man spoke.

"We are Aziel and Phoebe. You are Joseph, Mary, and Jesus. The doors to our hearts and home are open to you. Phoebe, take the mother and babe to their quarters. Joseph and I will put the beasts to rest." His quiet, genial authority made even a reply unnecessary.

Not until man and beast were refreshed and resting was there more conversation. Jesus slept in his crib. Joseph and Mary were seated at the board where they had eaten. The effects of the meal were removed and Aziel and Phoebe joined them around the table.

"I have tidings for you," Aziel stated in calm tones. "A messenger from Gaspar preceded you by three days. Much has happened in Palestine since your departure."

Joseph and Mary exchanged anxious glances, waiting silently. Aziel continued. "When the three men from the East did not return to tell Herod of the child that had been born king, he was angered and fearful. Then his courtiers told him of another child, one whom the prophets said would go before and prepare the people to receive the newborn king. This angered Herod all the more. He called his guards and bade them go to Bethlehem and slay this newborn king and his so-called harbinger. And in order to ensure their death, he instructed his guards to slay all male children in town who were not yet two years of age."

Mary sharply caught her breath. Joseph's face was pale. "All male children not yet two years of age?" Mary repeated incredulously. "Was it done?"

Aziel solemnly nodded his head.

Mary covered her lowered face with her hands. "How horrible!" she murmured. "The many mothers whose hearts and breasts are now desolate!"

She asked fearfully, "John and Elizabeth?"

"They are safe," Aziel stated.

"Zacharias had returned to the temple in Jerusalem," he continued. "Elizabeth went with him as far as Bethlehem and was back with Dalmatia. Zacharias knew of Herod's council, also that the guards had been dispatched, so he sent a swift messenger to warn Elizabeth. Dalmatia took Elizabeth and John and hid them in the hills. Often the guards pressed near, but Dalmatia's knowledge of the caves and hills eluded them.

"The chase in the hills became well-known so when the guards returned, they were afraid to report they had caught John for fear Herod would learn otherwise. They reported they had slain the infant king, but his harbinger they could not find. Herod angrily sent them to the tower in chains."

Aziel paused and fastened his gaze significantly on Joseph. "When Zacharias returned to the temple," Aziel began again, as if on a new theme, "he caused much concern among the priests. He refused to perform the animal sacrifice rites or to receive pay for the remission of sins."

A slow smile of admiration lit Joseph's face, a smile that was reflected deep in Aziel's eyes as he continued. "The priests, at least most of them, gathered in secret to determine what they could do. This attitude of Zacharias' threatened to disrupt the foundation of the temple and its source of revenue. They could, as priests, do nothing or the people's wrath would be upon them. So they decided to have Herod do it. Cunningly, they sent Herod the story that Zacharias knew where John was hidden.

"Herod's anger flamed anew. Immediately, he sent guards to the Temple, demanding of Zacharias the location of John. Zacharias replied that he knew not where the child could be found. The guards came the second time with the ultimatum that Herod would slay him if he refused to tell."

Joseph began to pale. Aziel reached across the board and pressed his arm. "Peace, my son," he said. Then he continued, "To the guards' amazement, Zacharias but smiled, replying that perhaps his own blood would help remove the revolting stench of the altar. The third time the guards returned, they had orders to slay Zacharias. They found him kneeling at the sacrificial altar. The guards knew he heard their approach, but Zacharias neither turned nor moved. With shaking hands one guard thrust him through, then they both fled in terror at that which they had done."

Joseph became rigid. Aziel's grip on his arm increased. Gazing deeply into Joseph's eyes, he stated, "It was Zacharias' desire to die thusly. His death was the beginning of the end of the animal sacrifice."

Joseph bowed his head in reverence to the spiritual valor of his magnificent friend as Aziel continued. "When the hour of salutation came, for Zacharias' daily blessing, the people gathered in the court. He did not come. After waiting long, the people began to call his name. Behind closed doors the guilty priests quaked at the results of their cruel cunning. The insistence of the people forced them to reveal what had happened to Zacharias. And there was grief, deep grief, in all the land.

"The next day, when the first courtiers came, Herod was already on his throne, as though he had been there all the night. More courtiers came, but Herod did not move. The king was dead! The death of Zacharias had been his last decree. His son now reigns in his stead."

Aziel paused and all were stilled with their thoughts. Mary's voice interrupted the silence. "Elizabeth and John?" she asked again.

"Fear not, my child," Aziel comforted. "They will soon be here."

"They are coming to Zoan?" Mary exclaimed incredulously.

Aziel nodded his noble, sensitive head. "Yes. Runners have already been dispatched for them

CHAPTER 14

A t dawn of the day following Elizabeth and John's
arrival, the entire household was astir. Aziel had
announced that on this day the instruction of Mary and
Elizabeth would begin. Leaving the house, they found a
world still moist from the kiss of night. Leaves, laden with
dew and stirring in the morning breeze, reflected golden
rays of the rising sun, making huge, glittering, living can-
delabras of the trees. The air was a cool caress, vibrant
with rich aromas fresh from the kingdom of energies.
Birds fluttered and soared, their throats bursting with the
joy of a new day.

They reached a clearing completely surrounded by
twelve giant sycamores. All twelve trees seemed the same
size and age; each, though far beyond its natural age, was
in perfect condition. The massive grandeur of the temple,
with its somber, lofty columns, had never filled Mary with
more awe nor made her feel more close to God as these
trees did. As they entered the clearing, she was struck by
the silence. It was as though the sentinel ring of trees completely shut out all sound. Even the cry of a bird penetrated not their vigil.

Beneath the north tree, Aziel stopped and motioned for
the others to seat themselves upon the ground. When he
spoke, his voice rang as though within a marble hall
instead of through an open space among sky and trees.
"From olden times, it was ordained that you should be
with us and in this sacred grove be taught. Time is meas-

ured by cyclic ages and the gate to every age is a mile-
stone in humanity's journey toward the Light. The touch
of time has opened another age. It will be an age of preparation; preparation for the Kingdom of Immanuel, which is
God in humankind. Your sons shall bear the tidings of the
age; they shall reveal to the people the power they have
hidden within. People now believe that the source of
power lies within the realm of their own strength and cunning because only in that realm can they see and touch.
But power from this source is sorely limited, while the
power of Holy Breath reaches beyond the concept of
human mind just as its nature is beyond the sense of touch
or sight.

"Sword and shield can be seen and touched. Holy
Breath can not. Yet a person, by using Holy Breath, may
remove from earth all sight and sound of sword and shield.
Confusedly, humanity mistakes action for power. Action
begets but action. Only in Holy Breath is power.

"In good will toward all, there is enough power to
destroy the armies of all nations; for goodwill is one of the
powers of Holy Breath. It cannot be seen or touched, yet it
is just as real as the power that moves the tides and turns
the days and brings to maturity these mighty sycamores."

Aziel paused and looked up and out at the trees. In his
eyes burned a glow of communion as though he sensed
from the trees an approving reaction to his words. To
Mary, the clearing was the circle of the zodiac and the
trees were its twelve signs with their respective purposes.
She wondered if the trees had been set out by masters of
the earth; or if nature, unaided by humankind, had erected
her own tabernacle. She thrilled as she thought of the masters who might have sat within their circle and the voices

that might have stirred their leaves.

And now the turn of time had placed her within this holy tabernacle to receive instructions in the work she was to do. Aziel had said the age of preparation had come. Humanity had climbed another rung in its ability to understand. Her son would teach that which humanity was now able to understand.

Mary pushed her fingers into the cool, pungent earth and gently patted it with reverent affection. A love for the earth, with its care and patience for human beings, welled in her heart. How she holds us in the palm of her hand, patiently waiting as we storm about, searching for the answer to that which causes our restlessness.

Mary was aware of a reciprocal caress from the earth. Her fingers tingled with its intimacy and in her mind, words began to form as though the earth herself was speaking. The words were, "I provide the arena for humanity's restlessness as long as it seeks the answer outside itself. When an individual finds the inner answer, I am no longer needed. You, Mary, shall be humanity's true mother. I am but a foster-mother. For through you comes he who shall guide humanity's awakening and to the end of its restlessness. Though you, shall humanity find peace and grow beyond need of me!"

Not until Mary felt a firm, warm hand upon her arm did she realize she was trembling. Turning, she looked into Elizabeth's calm, loving face and placed her hand over Elizabeth's in gratitude for her sweet thoughtfulness. Elizabeth patted her arm reassuringly and withdrew her hand for Aziel was speaking again.

"Your sons have a mighty work. Many want not the light. They love the dark and when light shines in the dark they comprehend it not. You must teach your sons and set their souls afire with holy love and make them conscious of their mission to humanity. They are revealers of the light, but they must first have the light before they can reveal the light. To many countries they will go and at the feet of many masters they will sit, for they must learn like other men."

Aziel turned his shining countenance toward Mary. "The only savior of the world is divine love and Jesus, son of Mary, comes to manifest divine love in the form of a man. Now love cannot be understood until its way has been prepared – and naught can prepare its way but purity. Neither is purity understood by humanity, but because of Moses, it is easier for humankind to understand than love."

Aziel now turned to Elizabeth. "Elizabeth, your son is purity made flesh that humankind may comprehend it, and thus the way be paved for love!"

He paused. Gazing out at the still, patient strength of the trees, his eyes grew misty with tears and his slender, erect frame trembled. "Alas," he sighed. "This age will comprehend little of the works of purity and love and their road will be a bitter one. But not a thought or word or deed will be lost. All shall be written upon the ethers and when the world, as individuals and as groups, is ready, the record will remain for them to read.

"Through purity and love, human beings develop eyes that see and ears that hear … and when they are ready, the ethers of Holy Breath will reveal to them the thoughts and words and deeds of your two sons."

Aziel's face lifted skyward and long he was silent, as though reading words already written in the Book of

God's remembrance. Mary was disturbed and somewhat frightened. It seemed that so much depended upon her wisdom – wisdom she felt not yet at all. Courageously, she interrupted Aziel's contemplation of the invisible. "So much depends upon my knowledge and there is so little that I know."

Aziel gently answered, "There is much time, my child, but perhaps there are certain things now you would ask of me."

Mary nodded. "What is this Holy Breath of which you speak?"

A smile of approval lit Aziel's face. "It is in the air that you breathe, in the winds that whip the trees, and in the blue of heaven's scope. The atmosphere upon and above and beneath the earth is like unto the waters of the sea. No where within the bed of the sea can be found a crevice where water is not. And wherever this water is, there is salt. Holy Breath in air is like the salt in the sea. There is not one single space in heaven or earth where it is not.

"Holy Breath is the symbol of the love of God. It is the power and the force that maintains all creatures. In it is the law of birth, growth, and fruition. An inexorable law that all life that ever was will live forever. Birth and death, as we know them, are but seasons toward life's fruition; fruition in the garden of awareness of our Godhood!

"Our salvation depends not on the caprice of a fickle God, as some would believe, but fixed forever in the air we breathe is the principle of protection and perpetuation. It is a principle that exudes from the heart of God and will wane not until all creatures are drawn back into this loving heart. Holy Breath is the invisible, living, constant presence of our Father God!"

Mary lowered her head and sobbed, so overcome was she by the glory of it all. When she could trust her voice, she asked again, "What must I do to learn the road toward fruition so I may guide the footsteps of my son?"

Aziel's answer came at once. "Study yourself. And after you have studied well, if you were to ask me what next, I would reply again, 'Study yourself.' When you well know your lower self, you know the illusions of the world. When you know your higher self, you know God and the things that cannot pass away. And only that which cannot change, cannot pass away, is real. And only in the real do we move and have our being."

Mary's face shone with gratitude and comprehension. That which she had heard found a permanent resting place within her heart and mind. One major question still remained. Again she lifted her voice. "Tell me, what is prayer? Is it to stand, or sit, or kneel and tell God of humanity's sins? Is it to tell the Holy One how great he is and how compassionate? Is God to be bought up by human praise?"

Aziel's face showed his appreciation of the daring profundity of his pupil. "The fount of prayer is the heart," he answered. "When you are separated from a loved one, is it not your heart that goes to him? The mother's heart yearns for her child; the heart of a wife aches for her husband.

"Each child needs to grow, to learn to walk alone, to discover him or herself, and from what is discovered to feel the urge to strive toward Godhood. Also, every person needs a stage upon which to have these experiences. This stage with its shifting scenes we call Mother Earth. Prayer is the *knowing* in our hearts that God waits behind each cloud and mountain, stream and vale. That God holds

forth a loving, helping hand as we move upon the stage of
earth. And *knowing* that from our own deeds and thoughts,
we turn God not away, but instead we turn ourselves away
from God.

"No, my child! Prayer is not in word and rite, but in the
focus of the heart." With a gesture of finality, Aziel said,
"This is but our first day." Then he smiled down at Mary.
"And for that first day, we have had enough."

Three years Aziel taught his pupils in the sacred grove
while Jesus and John waxed strong and splendid. Between
them grew a bond of affection glorious to see. John followed Jesus about, raptly attentive to every sound of his
exquisitely gentle voice. And Jesus, in turn, was at all
times exceedingly considerate of John's feelings and wishes.

They played not as other children play at games of
chase and battle, but seemed content to explore the forms
of life they found about them, whether belonging to the
kingdom of the animal or of the plant. For hours, they
would sit side-by-side, silently watching the sunlight upon
leaves, the wind in high grass, the antics of a fish or bees
at their work. And many times, they gazed together at the
same spot in space as though they saw interesting processions visible only to their holy eyes.

Aziel was happiest when he sat on his porch watching
them at their play. Once Mary remarked to him about his
seeming pleasure. With a contented sigh, he reached for
her hand and said, "Blessed are we among mortals for the
privilege of witnessing purity and love as they develop
and stretch their human wings."

One day Aziel announced that his lessons were closed
and they could go forth safely under the care of the Three

and the Seven. So Mary, Joseph, Elizabeth, and Jesus with his harbinger, set forth upon their homeward way. They went not by way of Jerusalem, for there Archelaus, son of Herod, reigned. They journeyed beside the Salt Sea into which empties the Jordan River. Near the middle of the sea's western shore was the fertile region of Engedi. Here, with Joshua, a near kin, they tarried awhile.

Engedi was famous for its fertile slopes, natural beauty, and wild goats. Also, it was here that David took refuge while fleeing from Saul. Near the house of Joshua was the cave where, while David hid within, Saul entered and was delivered into David's hands in accordance with the promise of the Lord. Also, near the house of Joshua were low cliffs from which issued the waters of a warm spring. When the young wild kids were old enough to drink, the mother goat herded them to this spring, forcing them to drink from its mineral-laden waters. From thence, Engedi received its name, which means *Spring of the Kid.*

For some weeks, the travelers rested, enjoying the green hills and Joshua's proud hospitality. Jesus and John daily roamed the country in a continual state of excitement at the interesting things they found, both at the dead coastline of the sea and within the thickly green crevices of the cliffs. But most of the time, they spent at the spring. The warm water with its metallic odor bubbling from the cliffs of clay constantly fascinated them.

One day, Mary and Elizabeth heard the rapid patter of little feet descending the path from the spring. They rushed out of the house and saw John approaching with reckless excitement. Both women clutched at the fear rising in their throats. John ran hard against his mother's knees and, clasping his chubby arms about her legs, threw back his head so that his dark shining eyes could look up into her face.

"Mother! Mother!" he exclaimed. "I made a dove from the clay at the spring and when it was dry, I gave it to Jesus for a surprise." He paused to swallow, gulping more air. "And Mother, Jesus held it in his hands, kissed it, and then threw it in the air. And it flew away! Isn't he wonderful!"

With another delighted squeeze of Elizabeth's legs, John turned and, stumbling up the path, hurriedly returned to his beloved Jesus, just as rapidly and excitedly as he had arrived. Mary and Elizabeth stared momentarily into each other's eyes and then, from sheer weakness and reaction, clasped each other and wept with relief and wonder at that which they had seen and heard.

It was decided that Elizabeth and John would remain in Engedi and that Joseph, Mary, and Jesus would follow the Jordan northward to the hills of Galilee and thence homeward to Nazareth. When the time of parting came, Jesus and John were quite manly. Not a tear did they show, but before Joseph's caravan was beyond earshot, both lads were weeping in their mothers' arms.

CHAPTER 15

For four years, Elizabeth remained in Engedi and gave John the lessons that Aziel had given to her. Also, she taught him Jewish law, the prophecies, and as much of the oral mysteries as his seven-year-old mind could comprehend. Together, they roamed the hills, John never tiring of the outdoors he loved so well.

Not far away was the cave of David in which dwelled the Hermit of Engedi. Since John first learned of his presence there, he had been consumed with curiosity to see this man living alone within a cave. Elizabeth attempted to discourage his adventurous interest in the hermit and thought she had succeeded until on his seventh birthday when she asked what would make him happiest, he replied that nothing could make him happier than to visit the hermit. Elizabeth agreed, hoping that the real thing would prove less fascinating that the product of his vivid imagination. So upon John's seventh birthday, Elizabeth prepared some food and they set forth for David's cave.

The cave was extensive with many lofty tunnels. Just when Elizabeth had decided the hermit was a myth, one of the tunnels spread out into a dome-shaped room. Clear yellow light came from somewhere among its ceilings; out of one wall, water sparkled and dripped into a small natural basin.

Beneath where the light from above shone the brightest, a man sat cross-legged upon a grass mat, writing upon a scroll. Long and lean, he wore but a loin-cloth, his skin gleaming with vitality and brown as a nut from the sun. For a moment, he continued to write. Then he turned his face to those who had entered his home. He smiled and motioned to a ledge upon which his visitors could sit. He walked over and stood above John, gazing deeply into the youth's upturned, fascinated face. Elizabeth watched him closely. This was no ordinary hermit. There was something about that which was happening that made her feel it had been foreordained, a fulfillment of things that were to be.

"John," the hermit said softly, as if to himself, "he who shall drink no wine and whose face nor head shall ever feel a razor's edge."

Elizabeth was amazed. How did this man know John's name and the prophecies concerning him?

The hermit sat upon his heels so that his eyes were level with John's. "Tell me, son," he inquired gently, "why this cave is known as David's cave?"

Confidently and instantly, John replied. "David was hiding here from Saul. Saul came into the cave to cover his feet, knowing not that David already was in the cave. Thus, according to the promise of the Lord, David's enemy was delivered unto him."

"Very good!" said the hermit. "And what did David do with his enemy?"

John glanced at his mother and straightway answered again, "When the Lord told David that he would deliver his enemy unto him, David was also told that he could do whatever seemed good to do. But instead of killing Saul, he only cut the skirt off his robe."

The hermit nodded with approval. Turning to Elizabeth,

"You have taught him well." Then back to John, he spoke. "The meaning of Samuel's books, as well as all books of the Lord, have several interpretations. For you, there is a special interpretation of the account of David, Saul, and this cave. To you, David is every person and Saul is a person's lower self that is hunting to take the soul. That which hunts the soul is anointed because there is naught that is not created of the Lord.

"David was told that he could do with Saul, his enemy, whatsoever seemed good to him when Saul was delivered into his hands. And when David had Saul within his power, he did not kill him, but he cut the skirt off his robe. In doing this, he took away Saul's dignity and importance. A dignitary in a short skirt has little authority among his subjects. His authority melts into subjection, which is the proper place for the lower self.

"We cannot kill our lower self, for it is anointed of the Lord; but we can deprive it of its authority and power, subjecting it to our will instead of being subjected to it. We do that by cutting off the skirt of its royal robe and exposing the lower self in its true light."

The hermit stopped and taking John's hand in his, he gazed into the clear, attentive eyes of the youth. "John," he said with the tender affection of a loving father, "you are to lead humankind to purity. Tell me what my words have meant to you."

John's eyes never wavered as he answered. "They were wonderful words and they meant to me that no one can love purity and hate impurity. Impurities are humanity's children that must be directed and controlled. To hate them in one's self or in others or to try to kill them outright makes tyranny out of purity."

John glanced adoringly at Elizabeth who sat delighted at the words of wisdom this hermit had drawn from her child. Then John turned back to the hermit. "Mother says that when we wave our virtue aloft and despise those dominated by sin we are only self-righteous, not virtuous."

The hermit released John's hand and bowed his head. His eyes were closed. To Elizabeth it seemed that the yellow light from the upper recesses of the cave moved down and pulsated in circles about his head. A sense of extreme well-being permeated her and radiated throughout the cave. John stared with fascination at the meditative hermit.

Soon the hermit stirred himself. He arose and moved to where Elizabeth sat. Kneeling at her feet, he lifted her skirt to his lips. Then he spoke. "Humanity shall be blessed forever because of what you have done with John. In no other way could he purify the hearts of humankind except through his love of them in spite of their error. Purity is not a cliff that we climb. It is the overcoming error and ignorance. Only through knowledge of their nature can they be overcome."

Inside, Elizabeth felt wonderful warmth. "Who are you?" she murmured.

"I am Matheno, priest of Egypt, master from the Temple of Sakara."

"Why are you here?"

"Awaiting John's arrival," was his startling reply for Elizabeth knew the hermit had been in the cave for many years.

The terrible ache, familiar to all mothers, rose in her breast. She realized her work with John was finished. Henceforth, his life and training would be under the guidance of this man, one of the masters of the earth.

Weakly, she arose. John glanced anxiously at her and then got to his feet. Elizabeth turned and walked slowly toward the mouth of the cave. John followed, but with every step, he looked back at the hermit. Matheno stood erect, the yellow light shining in his hair and his eyes smiling toward the stumbling John.

John clutched his mother's skirt. She stopped and looked down. Her heart had slowed its beating, for she felt the pull within her son, a pull he was trying heroically to overcome. "Mother," he pleaded, "could I not stay awhile with the hermit?"

Elizabeth forced a smile, though her face was like parchment. "Certainly, dear," she whispered. "As long as you like."

Then, turning, she hurried toward the mouth of the cave into the hard, real, light of day. John stood still, watching her retreating figure. "Mother!" he cried, the loneliness of a frightened child apparent in his tone.

Elizabeth turned. At the sight of her face his courage returned. "You will come see us, Mother?" he asked with concern.

"Often, my dear," she answered. "We will have many fine days together."

John smiled with relief. Elizabeth did not trust herself to remain any longer. Her eyes blinded with tears, she stumbled into the bright sunshine and along the path toward the house of Joshua. All the way, she continued telling herself that she knew John's life belonged to his work and to the world. But before Elizabeth had become the tower of strength and wisdom that she was, she had been a woman. And a woman she still was and the woman she was wept bitterly with every step she took.

For several weeks, Elizabeth remained in Engedi. Three times she visited John in his cave. The last time, she realized he had need of her no longer. John loved his Master, the wilderness, and their simple fare of nuts, wild honey, and locust pulp from the carob tree pods that served as their bread. So Elizabeth, knowing John was in the care of hands that had been prepared for him, went not again to the cave, but journeyed to Nazareth that she might be near Mary.

Mary was overjoyed at her arrival and listened in silence to her account of what had taken place with John.

Jesus had grown into the most beautiful child Elizabeth had ever seen. When first she saw him, the prophecy of Isaiah stood forth in her mind. "In that day shall the Branch of Jehovah be beautiful and glorious!" His eyes were a soft gray-blue, gentle and compassionate. His body was tall, straight, and slender. Above a clear, noble brow was long, fine, auburn hair that turned into a golden halo in the sun. His voice, though low and penetrating had a certain comforting vibration Elizabeth had never heard in any other voice.

He greatly loved the Vedic hymns and the Avesta, the Psalms of David and the words of Solomon. Long ago, he had fixed in his memory every single word of the Jewish books of prophecy.

One day, he walked into the room where Mary and Elizabeth were and moved his stool near his mother's feet as he was wont to do when he received her teaching. His expressive eyes were hurt and puzzled. The two women exchanged glances and waited for him to speak. Jesus spent much time with the rabbi of the Nazareth synagogue and he had just come from there.

Presently, he spoke. "According to the rabbi's words," he declared, his hands resting in his mother's lap and his eyes, wide with concern, turned up to her placid face, "God is partial in his treatment of his children and Jews are favored above all others."

"My Father is a just God. He could have no favorites. Samaritan, Greek, and Roman are just as much his children as the Jew." A heavy sigh shook his youthful frame. "It would be well," he continued, "if we could show the Jews that God has other children just as greatly blest."

He leaned his splendid head against Mary's knee. Lovingly, she stroked his fine curly hair. Suddenly, he lifted his face, a new thought reflected in its intensity. "Perhaps, I should go meet my kin in the other countries of my Father so that I could return and tell the Jews of the blessings that I find."

Mary smiled, a divine light in her eyes. "That you shall do, but the time is not yet come. So now to your books and when you next think of the rabbi and his words remember that if he knew our Father as you do, he, too, would realize there could be no favorites among his children. The rabbi is guilty of naught but ignorance and the true guilt will lie with you if you think ill of him."

Obediently, Jesus arose and departed. Neither Mary nor Elizabeth could look up from their work, so overcome were they by the destiny of this holy child beginning to stir within his young breast.

CHAPTER 16

It was the time of the greatest feast of the Jews and Joseph, Mary, Elizabeth, Jesus, and many of their kin went to Jerusalem. Jesus was eleven years of age and for days preceding their departure to the Holy City, his wondrous eyes shone with excited anticipation.

On their second day in Jerusalem, they were all in the crowded court of the altar watching the serving priest kill the lambs and birds and offer their burnt bodies in sacrifice for humankind's sins. Jesus sat next to Mary and she saw this face grow pale from shock at the sight of such wanton cruelty. He cringed at the frightened bleat of the lambs. She saw anger and resentment burn in his eyes and his sensitive face grow firm and set.

Mary feared for what he might do, for still fresh in her heart was memory of what happened to Zacharias when he dared challenge the temple customs. But she feared more the result of any attempt on her part to stop him.

Just as Mary feared, Jesus arose to his full height, his firm, slender shoulders erect, his splendid head thrown back, and his burning eyes fastened on the altar and the serving priest. His vibrant voice rang out as a bell. "What is the purpose of this slaughter of lambs and doves? Why do you burn their flesh before the Lord?"

The priest paused and a great hush filled the court. The priest was obviously ill at ease as he glanced appealingly behind him into the curtained Holy Place where sat other

priests, their presence hidden from the court. His manner
changed as though he had received instructions. He
became at ease and his attitude was that of humoring and
tolerating an unreasonable and obstreperous child. He
answered, "This is our sacrifice for sin. God has commanded us to do these things. God said that in these sacri-
fices all our sins are blotted out."

Jesus replied, "Where and when did God proclaim that
sins are blotted out by sacrifice of any kind? Did not
David say that God requires not a sacrifice for sin, that it
is sin itself to bring before his face burnt offerings of creatures for the forgiveness of sin?"

As if in echo to Jesus' words, there came from the outer
ring of the court another voice, vibrant with youth and
conviction. "And did not Isaiah say the same as David?"

Elizabeth, who sat on the other side of Mary, suddenly
gripped her arm with trembling fingers. "It's John!" she
whispered with incredulous joy. "It's John! And already
Jesus and he have together made their stand against the
error of the world."

Mary thrilled from head to foot. Looking back, she saw
the tall, splendid youth, his beautiful brown body covered
with but a loin-cloth, his long, dark hair and his eyes
gleaming in the sun.

The people began to murmur and stir. Upon the altar
suddenly appeared one of the higher priests. Quickly and
impressively, he pronounced a benediction so that before
disorder could occur the multitudes were dispersed.

Jesus made his way through the throng toward the
youth who had championed his cause. Mary and Elizabeth
followed as best they could. The excited people pointed

out Jesus to each other and whispered among themselves.

John remained standing at the outer circle of the court, Matheno towering quietly at his side. They were two picturesque figures, both personifying health and grace, and their loin-cloths in contrast to the colorful festal robes and headdresses worn by the celebrating multitudes.

When Jesus was yet at some distance, John recognized him and bounded to meet him. Clasping each other's arms, their faces beamed with their feelings. John was the first to speak. "I would have known that voice anywhere!" he exclaimed, his eyes glowing with pride.

Then rapidly and excitedly, John related to Jesus all that had happened in the past years, his outdoor life, his cave, his beloved Matheno, and that soon he was to study in Egypt in the Sakara Temple. Holding John's arms, Jesus listened, his eyes alight with interest and affection. Mary and Elizabeth stood nearby watching, their hands clasped hard beneath their shawls.

As John talked, he spied Elizabeth. He stopped in the middle of a sentence and stared directly toward her. With a sudden cry, he released Jesus and stepped quickly to his mother. Lifting her into his strong arms, he buried his face against her neck and squeezed until Elizabeth thought her bones would crack, though so exquisite the pain, she cared not if they did.

Including Mary in his embrace, he pivoted them all to where Matheno waited. Mary noted that Matheno rarely removed his gaze from Jesus and, lurking deeply in his eyes, she detected a reverence at what he saw.

Soon Mary and Elizabeth left Jesus, John, and Matheno and went in search of Joseph and their kin, for Anna and

Joachim, Mary's mother and father, had prepared a feast for them in the ancestral home of David. The feast was a merry one with much of the music Mary loved. Joseph was exceedingly tender and thoughtful, and when the time to return to Nazareth arrived, they had already begun their journey before Mary realized that Jesus was not with them.

Hurriedly, she and Joseph returned to find him. He was in none of the public places, so Mary sought the council of Halhul, high priest of the temple. Halhul immediately calmed her fears by telling her that Jesus was in the private court with the priests. But what he said next struck a new and greater fear to her heart.

Jesus' demonstration in the sacrificial court had aroused the concern of certain members of the priesthood, especially so when they learned he was son of the House of David and he of whom it was prophesied would become the promised Messiah. Such a person would have great influence among the people and, if such a person should challenge the profitable temple rites, it could prove very disastrous to their coffers. These priests were questioning Jesus to see to what extent his opinions were in antithesis to their own.

Halhul paused and sighed deeply, then continued. "The lad knows more of the true mysteries concerning the law than all the priests, and this does not please them. Knowing that I am a friend of yours, they have demanded that I obtain your permission to keep him a year in the temple with me. And during that year, I am to point out to Jesus the virtues of our interpretation of Jewish law over the interpretation that is his."

Mary was cold as stone with fear. "Will it not be dangerous?" she asked.

"Not so dangerous as taking him home. As long as he is here where they can watch his deeds, they will be unconcerned. But if he is beyond their sight, their concern might cause them to remove the thorn of his existence. Since Archelaus, son of Herod, has been sent to India, the Roman rulers could be easily influenced to dispose of any threat to the temple's subjugation of the people." Halhul sighed again, adding, "For the time being, I would suggest you permit him to remain with me. I will see that he comes to no harm."

Mary touched Halhul's arm, her heart filled with pity for this venerable patriarch. "What of you, Halhul?"

Halhul smiled faintly. "Fear not for me. Even though I have lost my influence as Chief of the Sanhedrin, the priests fear my favor among the people and would not dare cause me harm."

Mary reluctantly gave her consent and Halhul left to inform the priests and to bring Jesus to Mary. As the youth appeared, Mary was suddenly at a loss how to tell him he was to remain in the temple a year. "We were worried and have sought everywhere for you," she greeted, still groping for a way to tell him.

Jesus' face was sober. "I regret causing you concern, but you know I must be about my Father's business!"

Perhaps this attitude of Jesus would open the way. Mary quickly suggested to him, "Halhul desires that you remain a year in the temple. Would you wish to do so? Do you feel that in that way you would be about your Father's business?"

Jesus gazed directly into her eyes; his face became more sober and Mary felt that he could read the deepest recesses of her heart. It was she who was the child and he the parent. His eyes seemed to say, "I know your concern. I know the purpose behind your suggestion and I know the work expected of me by my Father."

Weakly she motioned to Halhul who had waited at a distance. When he joined them, Mary briefly told him that Jesus would remain. Then she turned to Jesus.

His eyes had lost their probing and were gentle and affectionate. With much warmth, he gathered Mary into his arms, holding her close. He kissed her cheek and whispered in her ear, "Fear not, lovely mother, and permit peace to live in your heart."

Mary released herself and fled. Never before had she experienced such strange emotion. Abruptly, Jesus was no longer a child; in his presence, she suddenly felt awkward and inadequate. At the outer gate, she ran hard into the protecting arms of Joseph. Firmly and quietly, he held her until her body ceased to tremble. Then gently, he tiled her face until he could look into her eyes. His only question was a lift of his delicately shaped eyebrows.

"It's Jesus," Mary murmured in reply. "Something inside him has suddenly grown up and he is to remain in the temple a year."

Joseph nodded, his dark eyes bright with understanding. Without removing his protective arms from his beloved Mary, he piloted her toward their waiting camels.

A year had passed. Again Jerusalem was crowded with people from near and far, come to attend the greatest feast of the Jews. Mary and Elizabeth again sat in the sacrificial court beneath the altar where a serving priest killed and burned the lamb and dove for forgiveness of the sins of those who had provided them and purchased the services of the priest.

Mary's questioning eyes finally located Jesus sitting near the altar. Halhul sat beside him, and Mary's heart ached at how hard the year had dealt with this splendid old man. His face was pale and drawn, but his head was still erect and in his eyes burned the same purposefulness.

Jesus' bearing and manner was that of a fully-grown man. But about both Halhul and Jesus, Mary sensed tenseness, as though they awaited an incident of possible unpleasantness. It was not long before that which she sensed became an actuality.

There was a pause in the sacrificial procedure and five priests in full regalia emerged from behind the veil of the Holy Place. They stationed themselves about the altar and one began to speak. "Last year," he began in sonorous, pompous tones, "there was a youth in this court who was unversed in the meaning of the rite of sacrifice. I see the youth is here again. It would please me to know if he now knows the significance of the sacrifice."

The priest looked down at Jesus. "Jesus of Nazareth," he said, rolling the Nazareth over his tongue with contemptuous emphasis as though the word Nazareth alone would hold Jesus in disrepute, "is it not written that the odor of burning flesh is pleasing unto the nostrils of Jehovah?"

Mary saw Halhul place his hand protectively upon Jesus' knee. Jesus covered Halhul's hand with his own, gave it a reassuring pat, and arose to his feet. Mary had never seen a more impressive figure, the most magnificent young man ever to stand within the temple walls. Loosely erect he stood, his noble head thrown back so that he could look up to the altar and the priests, his face poised and relaxed, even a trace of amusement in the curved corners of his sensitive mouth.

When he answered, his voice was calm, resounding clearly throughout the court. "Those who can read but the jot and tittle of the law are deprived of the spirit of its mysteries. What you say is true, but through gross living, you have blinded your eyes and dulled your comprehension. From the manner of your lives, you have hidden from yourselves the true interpretation of the law.

"It is also written that humankind was formed of two aspects. One is divine intelligence. The other is animal nature." The voice of Jesus suddenly began to ring with the sting of accusation. "It is the animal nature that was commanded to sacrifice. It is odor of a person's own animal flesh, being burned by the purifying fires of divine love, that is pleasing to the nostrils of Jehovah. Not this cruel, blasphemous, mercenary travesty with which you dare profane the temple of the Lord!"

Calmly, Jesus resumed his seat. Halhul's face was dead white. The priest who had spoken shook with the effort to hide his anger from the multitudes. Holding desperately to his dignity and employing the hypnotic tones of the priesthood, he attempted to disregard as insignificant that which had just happened.

"Often a youth," he announced deprecatingly, "from the zeal of his imagination arrives at the point where he thinks he knows more of the laws of God than all the priests of Israel."

Then he performed the rite of dismissal. But the crowds

did not leave immediately. The impressive words of Jesus had stirred seeds of doubt and the longer they milled, the louder and more significant were their questions of each other.

Halhul brought Jesus over to Mary and Elizabeth. After a brief but joyous greeting Halhul drew Mary aside. "Take Jesus and return to Nazareth at once!" he instructed her in guarded, ominous tones. "I will remain in order to learn what they intend to do."

Mary's face was pale and grave. "You are certain they will do something?"

"After that which happened," he smiled proudly, "they will be forced to or suffer the suspicions of the people. Just look at them now!" Halhul indicated with his eyes the various sober-faced groups in low-voiced conference.

"Go at once," he urged. "The anger of the priests might make them indiscreet and provoke immediate revenge, regardless of its effect upon the people." Chuckles emerged through his illustrious beard. "They expected quite a different performance from my pupil! Whenever they requested it, I reported that he was quite pliable and accepted readily the traditions of the temple." He shrugged his thin, aged shoulders, a roguish light in his eyes. "How was I to know he would prove defiant at the last?"

Again Halhul hurried Mary, so she called Jesus and Elizabeth and they made their way through the crowds to the outer gate where Joseph waited. Briefly, Mary related to Joseph what had happened. Though his face showed concern, his attitude suggested that he was well pleased.

As they rode through the streets of Jerusalem toward the Damascus gate, Joseph could hardly keep his fascinated gaze from Jesus, the boy who had suddenly grown into a tower of manly strength and wisdom. Jesus rode quietly and placidly, his eyes staring calmly at the passing scenes and sometimes gazing absorbedly into the open spaces above. Except for rest intervals, they did not break their journey until they reached their home on Marmion Way in Nazareth.

The next morning as Mary, Jesus, Elizabeth, and Joseph were discussing the warning Halhul had given them the day before, a servant entered with Halhul. He was so exhausted, he could hardly stand. Joseph assisted him to a comfortable seat.

Halhul explained, "The priests, led by Ananias, decided to bring Jesus to the temple to prove to the people they have no animosity toward him. Later, when the incident has been completely forgotten, they will find a way to dispose of him permanently. Jesus must not be taken to the temple."

Mary's voice was filled with concern as she said, "We are so grateful for the warning, but your journey has been too strenuous. Come, you must rest." She rose to help him.

Halhul quickly replied, "I could not trust anyone else with the message, but I must return immediately before I am missed."

Joseph stood and took his hand. "You shall have my speediest animals and most trusted men."

"A fresh animal, yes. Your men, no. You must not be identified with my absence from the temple."

Mary spoke again, "But you are so fatigued! It is dangerous to your health."

Halhul stood erect and looked with glowing eyes at

Jesus who also rose and stepped nearer to him, his face radiant with love and esteem. "My time is long passed," Halhul said. "I feel deeply blessed for this opportunity to protect our promised Messiah. Should it be my final act, it will bring to my life a special fulfillment."

He bowed reverently to Jesus, touched Mary's cheek lovingly, nodded to Elizabeth and Joseph, then strode from the room with renewed vitality. Joseph turned to the others and spoke in a voice that showed his concern for Jesus' safety. "Whatever we do, we must do at once."

Although Mary and Elizabeth joined Joseph in his concern, Jesus smiled to himself with quiet confidence. Suddenly, the servant entered again and announced, "There is a caravan approaching in the distance."

"It's too late!" Joseph cried. "They are already here!"

He hurried out to greet the new arrivals. Mary looked at Jesus who smiled reassuringly at her. He took one hand of both his mother and Elizabeth as though to comfort them.

Joseph burst into the room, his face beaming with joyful excitement. "It's Melchior!" he exclaimed. "Remember? He's the youngest of the three wise men. Gaspar has sent him to take Jesus to Parthia!"

He turned back towards the door. "Oh, what must he think! I did not even answer him. I just ran back to tell you!"

Melchior's laugh could be heard even before he entered the room. He and Joseph met in the doorway and he said, "Never has my presence been so enthusiastically received."

Mary moved towards him, her hands outstretched in

greeting. "Our apparent rudeness comes from our excitement that you have come at a time when you can fulfill
the desire you expressed to Jesus when he was only a babe
and you held him in your arms."

They clasped hands in greeting and Melchior turned to
Jesus. A reverence came into his manner and a respect into
his tone as he said, "The masters of many nations invite
you to come and receive the offering of their knowledge
so that you may return it to them as wisdom."

Jesus smiled and nodded his head as though nothing
unexpected was happening. He turned his attention to
Mary, his eyes glowing with love and tenderness as he
looked at her. Taking her hand, he led her away from the
others to the far side of the court. They looked deep into
each other's eyes for a long moment. Jesus placed his
hands affectionately on Mary's shoulders and spoke gently.

"While I am away, you will begin your part of our mission. When I entered your body, you were unified with the
light of the Holy Spirit. Within this light is all wisdom and
power. Whatever you need to know or do, turn inwardly to
it and it will respond."

Mary nodded, her face suddenly as radiant as his.
"Now I understand why I have felt the feelings I have and
know the truths I have known."

Pleased with her words, Jesus said, "I go now to share
our Father's blessings with people of other lands. When
this is done, I shall return and be with you in the fulfillment of my mission."

The next morning, another unexpected visitor arrived.
It was Joseph's sister, Sarah. She lived in a luxurious

home in Jerusalem with her husband, Benjamin, who was a very wealthy Sadducee, high priest and member of the Sanhedrin. Members of the Sanhedrin received commercial advantages from the Romans in return for which they were supposed to control all rebellious actions of the Jews.

Sarah was in tears and almost incoherent with fear and grief. Her husband had been imprisoned by the new Roman ruler, Archelaus, for warning Jesus and aiding him to escape.

"But it was Halhul who warned us!" Joseph said.

"It does not matter," sobbed Sarah. "Halhul died last evening from the strain of his journey before he could tell anyone."

Mary dropped her face into her hands. "Oh, dear Halhul! I was afraid for his well being, but I did not know he would give his life." Joseph encircled Mary with his arms and patted her gently.

Sarah continued in her grief stricken voice. "When the priests met the day before and decided to bring Jesus back to the temple as a captive, Benjamin spoke against it. Then when it was learned that Jesus had disappeared, Ananias was able to convince them that it was his kin, Benjamin, who was responsible. Ananias also convinced Archelaus that it was Benjamin. Not only has Archelaus imprisoned Benjamin for life, he has taken our home and given it to Ananias as a reward. What am I to do? My poor, poor Benjamin."

With her arm about Sarah's waist, Mary assisted her to bed. "Tomorrow," she assured her sister-in-law, "we will talk about what we can do."

Mary went to her own room. She knelt beside the bed.

Quietly, she spoke to herself. "Jesus said that if I needed
to know anything, I should turn to the light within me and
it would respond to my need. I now turn to it for guidance
in how to help Benjamin and Sarah."

She bowed her head over her folded hands and silently
waited. Ever since she had conceived from the holy light,
there had been a faintly visible radiance about her face.
Now as she prayerfully waited, this faintly visible radiance
became more intense and more vibrant until its golden
brilliance blurred the outline of her face. Then the light
decreased in brilliance until her face was normal. Mary
opened her eyes. They were aglow with a new wisdom, a
new gratitude, and a new confidence. Reverently, she
whispered, "I understand. Thank you. Thank you."

Mary entered Sarah's room where she was resting in
bed. Mary said, "There is something we can do for
Benjamin. It will not be easy, but if we do it properly, it
has the power to free him."

Sarah sat upright in bed. "Just tell me!" she exclaimed
excitedly. "Just tell me! I'll do it!"

"It's far easier to tell than to do. In the telling, it is simply this. You must love God and all humankind – and in
this case especially, you must love Archelaus."

Sarah was astonished and outraged. "Archelaus! How
can I love Archelaus after what he has done to my life and
to my Benjamin! He is our enemy, the enemy of our temple, and our Torah! Does not God expect us to hate those
who are against Him?"

With understanding patience, Mary persisted. "God
expects us to love others as he loves us, especially our
enemies."

Sarah was thoughtful for a moment. "How can we, as humans, love with God's kind of love?"

"Because we are created in his image and that includes his kind of love. Therefore, we already have the ability. All we need is to be willing to express it."

Again Sarah was thoughtful. "Even if I could, how would it help Benjamin?"

"Because this kind of love is all powerful, it can do anything. And the way it does it is to make all things work together for good. I do not know how it will help Benjamin. I just know that it will."

With an effort to sound purposeful, Sarah lay back in bed. "I will try! I will try!"

Mary kissed her forehead. "Each day we will try harder and harder." Softly, she closed the door behind her.

CHAPTER 17

E lizabeth had long passed the normal span of years and grew weaker each day. Mary was keenly aware of her waning strength and in every way that was unnoticeable to Elizabeth, she ministered to her needs.

"My time is near," Elizabeth calmly announced one day and added, "It is my wish that it happen in Hebron so that my body may rest near Zacharias' tomb." Then wistfully, she looked into the saddened eyes of Mary and said in tender tones, "It is also my wish that you be present when I go." Elizabeth lowered her eyes as though ashamed of the request and said, "I should not ask you to make such a wearisome journey for so dolorous a mission."

Mary's throat grew so tight she could not answer. Moving to where Elizabeth sat, she dropped to her knees, buried her head in the older woman's lap, and sobbed.

Dry-eyed and calmly smiling, Elizabeth stroked her lovely head, thinking of another time when Mary had sobbed in her lap, the day of her betrothal in the temple when she thought her emotional resentment toward Zaele had rendered her unworthy for that which was expected of her. Elizabeth reviewed the years, satisfied that Mary had proven herself worthy. She had completed all that was expected of her as the mother of the Messiah. She had guided him well. In the soil of her influence, the holy seedling had waxed strong in body, mind, and soul; and Jesus was now well on the road to his fruition. So much so

172

that he had been transplanted to the most fertile and hazardous forest of all – the forest where grow the trees of wisdom.

The first few days after they arrived in Hebron, Elizabeth seemed stronger, but soon her strength waned again. She had dispatched a messenger to David's cave near Engedi in hopes that John had not yet departed for Egypt and the Temple of the Nile where he was to spend many years. Mary was anxious that he be found, for it was exceedingly painful to watch her beloved Elizabeth's fading eyes brighten hopefully each time there was a knock at the door.

And then the day came when John was at the door! Blinded with joy, Mary arose to leave them alone, but Elizabeth stayed her. John's tall, lithe, magnificent body seemed out of place in the quiet stillness of this death chamber. His normally flashing dark eyes were dulled and saddened.

At the sight of him, Elizabeth brightened perceptibly, a smile stretching her pinched features. John knelt beside her bed and laid his cheek against her hand. Elizabeth twisted the fingers of her other hand into the abundant richness of his gleaming black hair. Her grip in his vibrant hair tightened as though from it she received the strength to speak.

"I sent for you, John," Elizabeth said, "so I might be certain that all the things that should have been told you by me were told. In a way, it is selfishness on my part because I want the peace that comes from knowing my work is finished."

She paused and drew a deep, tremulous breath. John was motionless. She began again in stronger tones. "The sages of the ages called you harbinger. The prophets shall look at you and say, 'He is Elijah come again.' Your mission is to prepare the hearts and minds of humanity for the coming of their Savior. Only through purity can they understand the words and the purpose of Christ.

"To teach people to be pure in heart, you must yourself be pure in heart, word, and deed. By being the example, the pattern, you provide others with that which they can follow. It is not enough to stand where the paths part and point the way. You must tread the way so that those who follow do so with the assurance that their teacher leads them over a familiar path.

"People grow to know the unseen, inner life by outer symbols that they can see and understand. It is your work to wash men's bodies free of the lower nature and the fumes of anger, greed, and lust so that they can see and comprehend the truth.

"Water is to be the symbol of this cleansing rite. Through this outer symbol, humankind will grow to know its inner meaning. You shall baptize with water, preparing all who are ready for him who shall baptize with the fires of holy love."

Elizabeth's words fell upon the stilled room as forms alive; and to Mary they remained suspended there as breathing, golden frames.

Elizabeth's fingers stirred in John's hair as though she sought a more secure grip, then she spoke again. "The call of death is for us all and it is always for the best, for where the problems are that we need most to solve, that is where our Father would have us be. My work here is done. I go to rest and then to other tasks. John, you must not grieve when I am gone. Grief for those who have departed through the door of death is but selfishness on the part of him who grieves.

"Death of a loved one should strengthen those left behind, should stir their awareness of the fact that they too must pass through its door, just as they entered through the door of birth. The separation of loved ones is often caused by divine purpose. When the loved one is removed, the direction of the remaining ones' stream of love is diverted. But this does not stop the stream of love; it continues to flow. And if the one who is left behind turns this stream of love toward God and toward the awakening of his or her own inner being, then there is greater benefit than if the loved one had remained."

Elizabeth spoke no more. Mary watched her fingers slide slowly through John's entangled hair and fall with gentle finality at her side. Her beloved Elizabeth had departed! Henceforth, that which they had done together she must now do alone. But in Mary's heart was naught but thankfulness that Elizabeth was now at rest.

On the return trip to Nazareth, their caravan rested outside Jerusalem. Mary, Joseph, and Sarah were seated in a tent waiting to be served a meal. Sarah said, "My heart aches that we are passing so close to Benjamin." She turned to Joseph. "Is it not possible for me to see him?"

Joseph answered, "Women are not allowed to see prisoners, but this is why we are returning by this route. I plan to see Benjamin."

Suddenly, there was the sound of authoritative voices outside the tent. A servant entered. "There is a messenger from Archelaus," he said.

Mary, Sarah, and Joseph looked at each other questioningly. "Show him in," said Joseph.

A soldier entered and announced to Joseph, "I am to bring you to Archelaus. I will wait for you outside."

When the soldier left, Sarah stared fearfully at Mary and asked, "Are we to lose Joseph, too?"

Mary was poised with deep faith. A smile of confidence radiated from her face. She affirmed, "We have enacted the power of divine love. Let us now stand still and watch it perform its mighty work!"

Joseph rose to leave and as he did, he and Mary exchanged deep looks into each other's eyes. He smiled and walked out the door to the waiting soldier.

In the court of Archelaus, Roman ruler of Palestine, Joseph waited quietly until he was summoned. The soldier who brought him there walked towards Archelaus, bowed, then moved forward and whispered into his ear. Archelaus immediately waved his hand to dismiss several others who were present, then turned his attention towards Joseph.

"Come forward, Joseph," he said. He waved towards a chair and Joseph seated himself. "I have heard that you are a pacifist," Archelaus began "and that you do not traffic in weapons, do not use slaves, and disapprove of the practice of animal sacrifice in your own religion. Is this true?"

Joseph nodded, somewhat puzzled by Archelaus' behavior. He was not sure what he expected, but it was not this. Archelaus studied Joseph a moment as though he was trying to make up his mind about what to say next. Finally, he spoke. "I have spent most of my life in India. My friends there pattern their lives after the teachings of Gautama Buddha who lived about 500 years ago. Since returning to Jerusalem to take my father's place, I have been very lonely."

Joseph glanced towards a corner where a small statue of Zeus, a bust of the Roman Emperor, and a statue of Buddha were on a marble table. He smiled understandingly at Archelaus, then spoke. "I have heard of Buddha and am familiar with some of his teachings."

Archelaus seemed to breathe a sigh of relief. "Then we can talk," he said. "Perhaps, you can make me understand the fanatical resentment the Jews have for the Romans. In India, I was taught just the opposite. The love of one's enemies is the crowing jewel of a good Buddhist's life."

Joseph answered, "A Jew cannot practice his religion under a foreign king because to him the only acceptable king is God."

Archelaus was silent, digesting what Joseph said. Then he asked, "If they will have no king but God, how will they ever *have* a king?"

"The promised Messiah will be their king. He will be from God ... holy and incorruptible."

"So, it's the coming of this holy Messiah that sustains their hate and constant resistance." Joseph nodded and Archelaus continued. "How do *you* feel about a Messiah being set upon a throne by force?"

Joseph's answer was spoken quietly. "It is of no importance what I think. The question is, how would the Messiah feel?"

Again Archelaus was thoughtful. Then his look darted straight to Joseph's eyes. "Do you believe your son Jesus is this Messiah?"

"He will prove whether he is or not."

Archelaus' voice was a bit sarcastic as he said, "It

would have been better for him and your people if he had
been confined to the temple long enough to prove himself!
Benjamin should not have warned him!"

Joseph's reply to Archelaus was more animated than
any of his words had been. "Benjamin? Benjamin did not
tell us of the danger to Jesus! It was old Halhul. The journey was too much for him and he died the same day he
returned to Jerusalem from our home."

Archelaus came abruptly to his feet. "What?" he strode
angrily around the room. "Ananias tricked me! I was a
pawn in his selfish scheme! But he won't get away with it.
When you leave here, you will take Benjamin with you.
His home and position will be restored to him."

Joseph rose and held forth his hand. "Thank you,
Archelaus."

Archelaus clasped Joseph's hand in both of his and
smiled. He seemed far removed at this moment from being
a Roman ruler. "There is nothing to thank me for, Joseph,"
he said. "I was deceived. It is I who should thank you. I
am looking forward to talking again with you. In the
meantime, it will be interesting to see what happens. As I
remember, Buddha said, 'Hatred can cease only by love.'"

Joseph returned his smile. "Yes, it will be interesting,
especially since our Messiah would not only agree completely with your Buddha, but would add that unconditional
love fulfills all laws, which includes exposing concealed
truths such as this deception by Ananias that has just now
been revealed."

The years slipped by, anxious years for Mary because
only at great intervals did information concerning Jesus
present itself. And the news that did come was always of
questionable authority.

Nazareth was on a trade route from West Arabia to Damascus. Merchants from Egypt, Asia, and India passed through Nazareth, some of whom were friends or kin of Joseph. It had long been customary for them to rest themselves and their caravans at Joseph's home. Many of these friends were familiar with the history of the birth and childhood of Jesus, and they happily related any story concerning him that they and heard in their travels across countries to the south, southeast, and southwest.

An aged cousin revealed that in India there were stories of how Jesus, after having studied the Brahman religion, repudiated its doctrine of the castes and taught the equality of all humanity. The Brahman priests were offended, so Jesus left their temples to live among the *sudras* and farmers, teaching them of equality. This so enraged the Brahman priests that they attempted to drive him from India. But their hirelings could find him not. He was never where they sought him. Not until he had finished his work there did he leave and then he completely disappeared.

Mary hugged closely every word, building around them additional detail fabricated by her anxiety for his welfare and her hopes for the progress of his work. As the years passed, she heard accounts of his work in the lands to the East and the South. With each story, she remembered the day Jesus sat at her feet and with such concern stated that he should go to the lands of his Father's other children so that he could return and tell the rabbi there were no favorites in the eyes of God.

One eventide as Joseph and Mary sat upon their roof watching the sun set behind the land of Philistia, Mary noticed an unusual tenderness in Joseph. He hardly removed his eyes from her face; eyes that were exceedingly bright in appreciation of what they saw. "No man was ever blessed as I have been blessed," he said with sober mien. "My life has been full to overflowing since first I looked upon the purity of your face. In the presence of you and while I yet live in this world, I want to speak my gratitude."

Mary took his hand. "Beloved Joseph," she said, "such words are unnecessary for you have *lived* your gratitude." She leaned her head upon his shoulder and added, "I, too, am blessed to have had at my side the strength and wisdom of your love."

Joseph did not answer but the abnormal light in his eyes burned even brighter.

The next morning, Joseph did not awaken from his sleep. In prayer, Mary expressed her thankfulness for the words they had spoken to each other the evening before. She knew now that Joseph had chosen that manner of bidding farewell to her and to his life.

Then a day came when a merchant delivered two letters, one from Jesus and one from Aziel. Mary feared the wild beating of her heart would never permit her to reach the sanctuary of her private chamber. Once there, she bolted the door. With the unopened letters clutched to her breast, she flung herself upon her bed and sobbed out her pent-up hopes and fears.

She knew not how long she wept, but when the sobs racked her no more, she felt as though a yoke upon her heart had been removed. With a new brightness, confidence, and strength, she tore the seal from Jesus' letter and began to read.

It was brief; each word she savored lingeringly. Thus,

she read:

Beloved Mother, from a traveler I received tidings that cause me concern for you. They were that our Joseph is no longer with you. I do not feel that you grieve or are disconsolate, but I feel that a word from me would comfort you. We both know his work in this earth-round was nobly done. Soon I will return to you and the people of my native land. And with me, I shall bring riches for all; riches that far surpass both the power of gold and the solace of human companionship.

That was all, but that little was enough. In it she read the fulfillment of her years of hope. He was coming home as the promised Messiah.

She moved to her window and gazed at the bright sunlight reflecting from the polished stone walks within the court. He was returning as the Messiah, but there was yet that of which the sun had spoken. As the Messiah, Jesus would lead humanity over the most direct path to God.

In her heart, Mary knew that the demonstration the sun sought from Jesus was that humankind need not die to reach God. Deep within the recesses of her heart an old uncertainty painfully stirred; an uncertainty born long ago of her inability to understand how her son was to achieve that which the sun proclaimed was within humankind's power and destiny. But on this day of days, she refused to permit that which she did not understand rob her of the joy of that which she did understand.

Tenderly, she laid the letter from Jesus aside and opening the other one from Aziel, she read:

Our teaching that began here years ago has been rewarded beyond my most hopeful dreams. For three days,

*your son Jesus abode with me. He has now gone, leaving
for you a letter that I shall send with this one.*

*He is truly wondrous! And all who contributed to his
unfoldment are surely blest, you above all. In every land
where there could be found wisdom, he has lived and
learned and taught. He stopped here as he was returning
from a meeting with the seven sages of the world.*

*In every age since time began have seven sages lived.
At the turn of every age, these sages meet to observe how
far toward love and righteousness the races have pro-
gressed and to plan that which is suited best for their
progress in the coming age.*

*First the sages needed to be certain of their man. First
he must be subjected to the seven great tests. The seven
battles must be fought, the seven victories won. These
great tests Jesus fought and conquered. When they were
over, the sages spoke as one. "Jesus, you man from
Galilee, chief of all the sages of the world, in recognition
of the wisdom which you bring to humanity, we crown you
with the lotus wreath."*

*Then all the sages bowed their heads and reverently
murmured with one accord. "You are the Christ, forever
more! Thus, the chosen of heaven became the chosen of
earth and every living creature said 'Amen.'"*

For days to come, Mary was conscious of naught but
the heavenly song of rejoicing voices.

CHAPTER 18

Throughout all Judea, there moved the story that a wild man had suddenly appeared on the banks of the Jordan. He came from the hills of Engedi. His home was the cave of David. He was clothed with camel's hair and about his loins he wore a girdle of skins and he ate only wild honey, fruit, nuts, and the bread of the carob tree.

To everyone who crossed the Jordan ford near Bethabara, he said, "Behold, the King has come! The prophets told of him, the wise men long have looked for him. Prepare yourselves to meet the Lord!"

When Mary heard about these things she knew it must be John who had returned from Egypt to begin his ministry as the harbinger of Jesus. She was filled with joy and immediately left for Bethabara that she might see him at his work.

In thousands of years, the River Jordan had changed but little. It separated Galilee, Samaria, and Judea from the rest of the world. It offered nothing to anyone but danger and difficulty, perplexity and trouble. Its whirling eddies, treacherous fords, shifting bottoms, and changing currents were to Mary symbolic of the nature of our lower selves, through which we must cross if we are to reach the peace of the promised land.

As Mary approached its swirling yellow flood, she was astonished at the multitudes of people thronging its bank. Leaving her caravan with its attendants, she made her way

on foot to where she could get a glimpse of John. When at
last she was near enough to see him, his magnificence left
her breathless. He stood upon a promontory, his large body
beautifully molded and shining like highly polished
mahogany. His dark hair and face that had never felt a
razor's edge gleamed in the sun at his every move. Lights
flashed from his deep brown eyes as he preached to the
people.

Before Mary realized it, tears were in her eyes and she
was saying over and over, "Oh, Elizabeth, if you could
only see him!"

When she had calmed herself, she moved closer that
she might hear his words. His voice was strong and clear.
"Come unto me and in the waters of this stream be washed
that you may be ready to meet him who comes after me,
the latchet of whose shoes I am not worthy to unloose.
Wherein I baptize you with water, symbolic of the cleansing of the soul, when he comes, he will cleanse in Holy
Breath and purify in the fires of divine love.

"This fan is in his hand and he will separate the wheat
from the chaff and will throw away the chaff and garner
every grain of wheat. This king of humankind to come is
your savior. He is the Christ! Hearken to the voice crying
in the wilderness. Prepare yourself for him who comes, for
the kingdom of heaven is at hand!"

Near Mary, a wide-eyed young shepherd asked of a
local farmer, "Has this strange man been long here? Does
anyone know his name?"

"For many months," replied the farmer. "He has spoken
in Jerusalem, Bethany, Gilgal, and Jericho. No one knows
his name. He calls himself the harbinger of the Lord, but
there are those who say he is Elijah come again, he of

whom the prophet Malachi wrote."

The eyes of the awe-struck youth widened. "Have any of the people accepted this baptism rite?" he asked.

The farmer nodded solemnly and answered, "Many. Soon he will enter the water and you shall see!"

Mary was moved by the wonder in the young shepherd's clear eyes.

John's words became more fiery. Some of the people were stirred and asked, "What must we do to prepare the way for him who comes?"

John replied, "Practice helpfulness to all. Spend not all you have upon yourselves. If you have two coats, give one to another who has no coat, and give a part of your food to those in need."

A publican advanced and asked, "What must I do?"

"Be honest in your work," John answered. "Do not increase for selfish gain the tribute you collect. Take no more than your king demands."

Two soldiers approached, their faces ruddy but anxious. "And what must we do?"

The harbinger replied, "Do violence to no one. Use not your authority for personal greed and be content with the wages you receive."

John tossed aside his cloth of camel's hair and dressed only in a loin-cloth of skins, raised high his arms. "Those who would be free of the empty husks of desire and greed, follow me into the purifying waters of the Jordan!"

Stepping down from his promontory, he strode toward the stream. In John had man attained physical perfection. His wide, brown shoulders and head of lustrous hair

showed majestically above the heads of those who followed. None who followed approached him in strength,
health, or comeliness. Many were deformed, lame, and
blind.

To Mary the conviction came that only in a perfected
physical body, one's earthly vehicle, could the fullness of
life be experienced as it was planned. The laws governing
the physical body existed not as punishment for indulging
in the appetites of the flesh, but existed to guide people
toward fuller realization of this wonderful gift.

The waters of the Jordan were almost hidden by the
variously colored garments and headdresses worn by the
throngs that followed John into the river. It was a sight so
spectacular and impressive that the colors and figures were
blurred by the tears in Mary's eyes. John's clear voice
came ringing up to her.

"In the same waters, across which Joshua led into the
Holy Land those whom Moses had prepared, I prepare
you. I prepare you for the One to come, the One who can
lead you into the very presence of God."

Mary watched the reactions of the baptized people.
Some were silent with reverence. Some were frightened.
And some, stirred by their emotions, chanted and sang
praises to God and the forthcoming promised Messiah.
She knew she would be unable to get near enough to
speak to John so she retired to her caravan, planning to
return early the next morning before the people gathered.

But when early the next morning she returned, it
seemed there were more people than on the previous day.
Apparently, everyone else had made similar plans and others were continually arriving. John was again on the
promontory. He paused abruptly in the midst of his speak-

ing, one arm remaining suspended with his hand pointing
out over the heads of the assembled multitudes.

Mary's eyes followed the direction of his attention.
What she saw completely took her breath away. Walking
slowly toward John was the most handsome man Mary
ever had seen. He was tall, slender, and erect and moved
with graceful ease. In the sun, his golden hair flowed back
from the noblest of all brows to rest upon strong, straight
shoulders. His blue eyes sparkled and flashed. The gentleness about his countenance bespoke an infinite strength.
The texture of his skin was much finer than other men's
and from it came an indefinable glow that was felt rather
than seen.

As he moved toward John, he glanced into the faces of
the people he passed. In his eyes was the same expression
Mary had seen in the eyes of an anxious mother as she
gazed down at the sleeping form of a sickened babe: love
and care, free from the awareness of self. Mary knew it
was Jesus, but so enthralled was she by his beauty of
form, color, and manner that she could do naught but stare
in wonder.

At the foot of John's promontory, he stopped and turning his face up to John, he spoke. "I would be washed in
water as symbol of the cleansing of the soul."

That particular resonance in his voice that had always
gladdened Mary's heart was greatly enriched. Never had
she heard a more beautiful sound. In addition to that certain quality, Mary had remembered from his childhood
that there was something else that struck a familiar chord;
something she had not associated with Jesus. His was the
same as the voice she had heard from the sun! It had the
same gentle authority, the same modulated resonance. She

could not believe it was the same voice, yet something inside her told her it was. Also, that indefinable glow from his face! She had seen a similar glow, radiating from the rim of the rising sun.

John's arm had remained extended all this while. Slowly and reverently he lowered it, his eyes afire with joy and zeal "You are the one for whom we wait," he said. "You do not need to wash for you are pure in thought and word and deed. If you need to wash, then I am not worthy to perform this rite."

A faint smile of understanding and affection moved across Jesus' face. In gentler tone, he requested, "Suffer it to be that we may fulfill this rite of righteousness. What I ask of others, I too would do. And it follows that what I do, others can do also."

John did not answer, but led Jesus down into the river. There he baptized him in the name of the Triune God who sent him forth to manifest the Christ in humankind. There was a hush through earth as these two men came out of the stream. Two magnificent men: one dark, powerful, and zealous; the other ruddy and golden, and there was in his calm and poise unfathomable strength.

All the rays of the sun suddenly seemed concentrated upon Jesus' head. His face was almost hidden in vibrations of streaming light. From the heavens, Mary heard a voice. "This is my beloved Son, in whom I am well pleased!"

On reaching a high place, Jesus stopped, and lifting his voice spoke to the hushed and hopeful multitudes. "Nothing can compare with the glory that is hidden from your gaze by the clouds of impurity. The kingdom of heaven is at hand, closer to you that the breath you breathe. With your purity, I shall light the lamp of love and the light of this lamp will lead your feet to the kingdom of heaven. For awhile, I must go into the wilderness. But soon I shall return and gather unto me my own!"

Jesus turned and disappeared into the crowd. Mary's heart was sick. She feared she had lost him. Suddenly, that wondrous voice spoke. "You must always seek me by your side, little mother!"

Mary turned and there he stood. She rushed into his arms and he held her fast. "I was almost home," he whispered in her hair, "when you departed for the Jordan. Long had I yearned to tread again the hills of Galilee, so that I did. You return to Nazareth and after certain of my work is done, I will join you there."

Jesus gently released her and was gone, but Mary knew that never again would she be alone. How sweet had been his voice when he called her, "Little mother." Suddenly, Mary's mind was again aflame! Only once before had she been called "little mother," and that was by the voice from the sun as it told her she was capable of being mother of the One who was to overcome death!

CHAPTER 19

B ack in Nazareth, Mary waited for the arrival of her wondrous son. Often in her life, she had thought her heart filled with joy, but the joy she felt now was almost more than she could bear. There were times when she thought her heart would burst, but always like a steadying hand was a sense of overwhelming humbleness that she had been chosen to be his mother.

There were many reports of John from the camps, but none reached her of Jesus. Never before had the country been so animated and communicative. If one heard of an incident that he or she believed was new, the story was quickly passed on to others. There was no person more envied than the teller of tales from the Jordan camps.

Forty days passed and still there was no report of the reappearance of Jesus. Strong was her conviction that naught could happen to him except that which was planned, but as the days passed this conviction wavered more and more.

One day when the suspense seemed unbearable, in an effort to divert her attention, Mary walked up Marmion Way toward Nazareth's little market place. Desperately, she attempted to absorb herself in selecting a ripe melon, but to her they were all alike. Just melons. Fearing that friends would discover the extent of her distraction, she determined to leave the market place and go directly home.

As she turned from the melons and the solicitous ven-
dor, there came the sound of running feet. Down through
the middle of the street, his robe and headdress sailing
behind, came a local tradesman. Panting and wide-eyed
and trying to hold on to a vestige of the dignity such information as he bore warranted, he came to a halt in the center of the stalls. "Jesus, the Christ has been found!" he
announced with all the pomp he could muster.

Mary was suddenly lighter than air. "At last!" echoed
and re-echoed through her being.

"He came down from the wilderness of Judea," continued the proud messenger, "where he had fasted for forty
days. He teaches now with the wild man, his harbinger, at
the Jordan!"

The tradesman suddenly recognized Mary in his audience. Automatically, he bowed and uncovered his head.

"I especially am grateful for your tidings, Amoon,"
Mary said. Glancing happily about at her attentive friends
and kin she added, "Soon now, he may come to Nazareth."

Unfettered joy rushed back into her heart, and closing
her veil that it might not be too obvious, she hurried home.

A few days later, just at eventide, Jesus and six disciples arrived. The expression that came in his eyes when he
looked into Mary's happy face was all the greeting she
could ever ask. "Little mother," he said, "these are men
who have chosen to follow me in my work."

He introduced them. "This is Peter and his brother
Andrew; Phillip and his brother Nathaniel; James and his
brother John. We would all abide a while with you."

Without instruction on her part, the members of Mary's
household sped to prepare for the comfort of the wondrous

Jesus and the men of simple garb who were his guests.

The next morning as they broke their fast, Mary saw a sadness deep in Jesus' eyes that was not there the day before. The disciples departed for a walk, leaving Jesus and Mary alone. For a while they sat in silence, then Jesus turned to Mary.

"Little mother," he said gently, "our beloved John we will see no more. With the human mind, it is hard to comprehend that his work is finished, that so many years were spent in preparation for so few months of service."

"What has happened to John?" Mary asked apprehensively.

"At Machaerus, he openly shamed the tetrarch for his lustful relations with the wife of his own brother. John was arrested and imprisoned." Jesus paused, the sadness burning deeper in his eyes. With a sigh, he added, "Our John shall suffer a very ignoble death at the hands of those he accused."

Mary was stricken. She could not believe it. "You are certain?" she asked. "There has been no word of his arrest."

In reply, Jesus stated simply, "Last night I was with him in his cell. We talked all night. Not an incident of our childhood was forgotten."

It did not seem strange to Mary that Jesus, though he retired in Nazareth, spent the night at Machaerus in a prison cell with John. In her mind, she saw them as they talked. "And John?" she asked, a pain deep in her breast. "Does he know?"

Jesus nodded. "Yes. At first he was bewildered. But before I left, he understood that it was according to the plan."

Mary grew cold. A surge of gratitude moved through her that Elizabeth had been spared this experience.

At that moment, Peter returned. Approaching Jesus, he said, "Master, as I walked I met the ruler of the synagogue. He asked me who you were. I replied you were the Christ of whom the prophets wrote." His eyes lowered as he finished. "The ruler bade me tell you to come to the synagogue that he might hear your plea."

Jesus nodded his head in acknowledgment, a slight smile of amusement on his lips. Touching Mary's shoulder affectionately, he arose. "I would retire to my chamber for a while," he stated and departed.

In the evening, Mary and Jesus sat alone in the inner court. The ruler of the synagogue who had spoken to Peter entered and was graciously received. In tones of authority, he asked for proof that Jesus was the Messiah and why he went not to the synagogue where he was bidden.

Patiently, Jesus answered. "No man bids me come and go. My ministry comes not from priests. The demands of humankind are not for me. To God alone do I answer."

Gazing significantly into the priest's astonished face, he continued. "From whom did you obtain the right to ask for proof of my ministry? If proof you sincerely seek, then follow me and you will find it in my words and works."

Confounded, the ruler took his leave.

Mary's heart was full and she yearned to express its fullness with song. Obtaining her lyre, she returned to the court and in the soft light of evening sang her beloved songs of Solomon and David.

Hearing her, the six disciples came out from the house and sat in the grass at her feet. They were enthralled, Peter

especially, for his rugged fisherman's heart had never
before felt the caress of voice and song so sweet. To these
simple men of soil and sea, Mary's beauty and gentle sincerity, plus being their Master's mother, made her divine
in their eyes. And Mary, in full measure, returned their
love and admiration.

The next day, throngs of townspeople gathered in the
ante-court waiting for Jesus to appear and speak. Upon the
roof he appeared and, with eyes filled with tenderness,
gazed down into their anxious upturned faces. Then he
spoke.

"A prophet is without honor in his own homeland
among his own kin. When my works in other towns have
won the faith of others, then will I speak in Nazareth.
Good will to you, my friends and kin, and I bless you with
a boundless love."

No more he said and the throng, marveling much at his
words, moved away.

North and near to Nazareth was Cana where a wedding
feast for Mary's kin was held. She longed to attend and
prevailed upon Jesus and his disciples to accompany her.
Before the feast was over, the wine did fail. Mary was disturbed for her kin and said to Jesus, "What shall we do?"

Smiling at his mother's concern, he said, "All creation
is formed of the same substance. That which makes one
form different from another is but the power of holy
thought. Have six pots of water brought forth, a pot for
each of my disciples, and I will show you and them what
holy thought can do."

This was done and as Jesus stood apart in silent
thought, the water changed to wine. The servants passed

the wine and it was claimed the best of all. The people were amazed. And within the disciples arose a new dignity and in Mary's heart stirred a new joy.

The day they returned to Nazareth, Peter approached Jesus. As though apologetic for his tremendous size, he remained at a distance and, because of his uncertainty concerning that which he was about to speak, his gaze remained at Jesus' feet.

"Master," he said, "my brother and I and James and John are fishermen. Our nets are untended and rot in the sun." Peter shifted uneasily before continuing. "While you are here, could we journey to my home in Capernaum and tend the nets? We would not be many days gone?"

Mary's heart swelled with affectionate understanding for this strong man, so free from guile, now torn between a desire to please his master and a natural anxiety for his beloved nets. And in Jesus' eyes, she discerned the same feeling that was hers.

"Peter," Jesus said, and strong in his voice vibrated that stirring quality that Mary loved so well, "no longer will you stretch your nets for fish. All of you are now fishers of men. We will go to your home. There you may repair the nets so they may be used by your friends. Then along the shore, we will cast our nets for the lives of humankind."

Peter's head came up and his eyes shone like those of a delighted child. The other five, ill at ease in the background, now joined their elected speaker, relief and joy flickering from face to face.

To Mary, the glances they exchanged were beautiful. Peter, in his enthusiasm, announced to them as though they had not heard. "Not only are we going home, but we

are going home with him. All Capernaum and Bethsaida
shall see and hear our Master!"

Peter's joy-filled eyes suddenly fixed themselves upon
Mary and she saw their brightness dull. He gazed about at
the lofty ceilings and marble floors of the ancestral home
of the lineage of David known as the Carpenter Tribe,
builders of temples and synagogues. He glanced into
Mary's face, then to Jesus and back to Mary, and said,
"My home is miserable compared to yours." He paused as
though his courage failed.

"Yes, Peter?" Mary encouraged gently.

"We would try to make you comfortable," he muttered.
And then declared with an honesty of feeling that would
not be denied. "You have been so generous to us."

Within the framework of those simple words glowed a
picture of warmth and beauty that Mary saw reflected in
every face. There could be no earthly treasure, she
thought, more precious than the genuine feeling she read
in every heart.

She turned to Jesus. He nodded his head, moved to her
side, and placing his arm about her shoulder said, "Yes,
we would have you go with us."

With a slight, but significant clasp, he added. "This is
the beginning of my ministry in this my native land. It is
fitting that you witness the result of that for which you
have spent your life."

CHAPTER 20

The snug neatness of Peter's home on the north side of
Galilee gave Mary a sense of mellow comfort. They
arrived in Capernaum after dark. Andrew, James, and John
went on to their homes nearby and Mary, Jesus, and the
other two disciples remained in Peter's home.

Shortly after a lamp had been lit, the door flew open
and in rushed young Elizabeth, eyes like stars and calling
for Peter with every breath. Gathering her into his arms as
though she was a child, Peter joyfully swung her back and
forth. To Mary, Elizabeth's love for Peter was plainly dis-
cernible, as obvious as was Peter's unawareness that it
existed. Watching their greeting, Mary was at once happy
and sad. Happy at such genuine demonstrations of spontaneous joy from both of them and saddened by a fear that
this woman's love, shining so brightly from Elizabeth's
face would never be fulfilled. Peter neither saw it nor
would understand it if he did.

On this night of their arrival, before Jesus went into his
room, he said to Peter, "Until you have repaired your nets
and assigned their use to others, I would prefer my presence here be unknown. Let all know when you are to
assign the nets and, on that day, I will speak. Until then,
suffer me to remain undisturbed in my room." Turning to
Mary and Elizabeth, he added with a smile, "If the time
seems long, fret not, for there is nothing I will need."

During the first days, Elizabeth was much in the house,

cleaning and cooking and she and Mary soon were fast
friends. "You're so beautiful!" Elizabeth would exclaim at
most unexpected times.

Mary always kissed her happily, saying, "We can see
beauty only if we ourselves are beautiful."

On the third day, through a window, they watched the
gathering crowds. Peter, Andrew, James, and John were
finishing the last of the nets. Azzah, a powerful man and
friend of Peter, had remained all day each day since he
learned that Peter was to give away the nets. And each
day, Azzah, along with others, inquired of the weaving
fishermen concerning the stories they had heard of the
arrival in Jerusalem of Judah's king, the promised
Messiah.

"He is truly Emmanuel!" Peter always replied. "But not
until we assign the nets can you know more, and then you
will know all there is to know."

Mary and Elizabeth saw Peter arise. His glance at the
others ascertained that they, too, were finished with the
nets. "It is time!" Peter announced to the increasing
crowds and hurried into the house.

Entering, he approached Mary, his face alight with
excitement. "We are ready," he almost whispered. "Shall I
call the Master?"

Mary nodded her head. At that moment, Jesus spoke
through the door. "When you have assigned the nets, bring
the people to your boat where it lies upon the beach."

Glancing excitedly from Mary to Elizabeth, Peter
turned and ran from the house. They watched his huge figure returning to the nets where Andrew, James, and John
awaited. In private he spoke to them, and then mounting a

bench, he raised his arms to the multitude. There was silence.

"It is agreed among us that one of you shall be responsible for the others. Unto Azzah shall all the nets be assigned. He, in turn, shall choose those who are to work with him. This we do if Azzah agrees that when the fish are scarce, no one shall go in need."

Proudly and solemnly, Azzah agreed. Then a clamor arose for the promised tidings concerning the Messiah. Peter glanced uncertainly toward the house. Then in a loud, confident voice, he exclaimed, "Follow me!" Stepping down from the bench, he strode toward the sea. Following him came Andrew, James, and John, and after them, came the multitudes. Mary and Elizabeth, hand in hand, followed the multitudes.

Upon the deck of Peter's beached boat stood Jesus, erect and still; a gentle wind stirring his fine, luxuriant hair as it gleamed golden in the bright sun. Mary thrilled from head to foot at the impressiveness of his tall, slender figure outlined against the clear, green waters behind him; green that changed to violet, purple, and blue beneath the shadowed fingers of floating clouds. This background of liquid colors made the brilliance of Jesus' blue-gray eyes flash and sparkle as his gaze moved across the expectant faces gathering around him in such respectful orderliness.

Standing at the rear of the crowds, Mary felt as though she was witnessing a scene in an amphitheater. It was the first time she had been down to the water's edge. She was fascinated by the pink hue of the beach caused by millions of tiny shells. She raised her eyes to gaze over the verdant sweep of the Gennesaret plain gradually rising from the Sea of Galilee, then lifted her eyes higher to the dark precipices of the Robbers' Gorge disappearing back into the western mountains.

In every direction she turned, the world was a stage that had been waiting and preparing itself for this scene, from the ageless shells beneath her feet to the wind and clouds that tiptoed by with as little distracting motion as possible. She thought this impression must come from the feeling within her own heart. For all her life had been spent in preparation for the drama that was about to begin. The first scene would be the opening of Jesus' ministry among his own people. How near would this play reach her dreamed-of climax? Would this wondrous man, with eyes so soft and face so strong, fulfill that of which the Sun spoke? Would he demonstrate to man that there is no death?

An exquisite thrill of anticipation moved through her. Jesus was about to speak. He had moved out to the prow of the boat. A wide sweep of his eyes included every person within the circumference of his radiant presence. Lifting his glorious voice and with the simplicity of one who knows and the assurance of one who has seen, he spoke.

"It has been written that one would come to deliver the people from their enemies, one who would be king, king of the Jews. Many have thought their enemy was the Roman yoke and that the king to come would remove from them this tyranny. But as long as there are Jews who, for greed, would keep in bondage other Jews, the removal of the Roman yoke would only make room for another of Jewish make.

"You people of Galilee, your enemy is not the publican who collects the Roman taxes, the Roman solider who confiscates your beasts and despoils your women folk. Your enemy is the lower self of all humankind, Roman and Jew alike. And not until this lower self is overcome, will humanity be delivered from its enemies.

"That is why this enemy is called the 'enemy within your gates.' And it is why each individual must deliver him or herself from the enemy within. The animal nature of humankind transmuted by the fires of purity upon the altar of humanity's love of God is the only rite of animal sacrifice pleasing to heaven.

"Not by force of arms can the yoke of nations be removed. This but exchanges one neck for another within the yoke; a form of activity belonging not to the progress of humanity's awakening."

Jesus paused. His words were not what the people had expected to hear. They shuffled uneasily.

Huge, powerful Azzah raised a respectful voice. "How, Master," he asked, "are we to overcome the enemies within Palestine and the enemies within ourselves?"

"Each person," Jesus answered, "is divine, created in the image of God. And from this divinity comes a voice; a voice that points the way to his or her awakening. If you go inside your being, shut the door, be very still and listen, you will hear this holy voice. Follow its guidance and it will lead you to the discovery of your divinity. You will then live in the kingdom of heaven, which is *ever* at hand.

"Thus it is written, 'Vengeance is mine, says the law of the Lord.' To the extent that you permit your Father to be the judge, to that extent will you prosper. Because then you subject your will to his and in his will is naught but justice and love."

Jesus paused and again Azzah spoke. This time there was a light of understanding in his eyes and an enthusiastic lilt to his voice. "How can we know, Master, when the enemy within ourselves has been overcome?"

"When no longer do you judge another! A heart that is free from accusation and condemnation is a heart that has overcome anger, greed, and desire, and therefore it is a pure heart; a heart wherein the Christ may abide. Thus you are reborn while you are yet alive."

Again Azzah's voice came forth. "Evil exists because we see its power among us. Tell us how best we can fight this power of evil."

Jesus replied, "All there is was created by God, and all there is, is good. But all things have colors, tones, and forms. These, though good within themselves, when mixed in discord with their nature produce inharmonies that people call evil.

"Everyone has their own will and can mix God's good things in a multitude of ways. Thus each person creates his or her own devil and then becomes afraid of it and flees. The devil follows, casting the one trying to escape into fires of torture. Since both the devil and the fires are created by a person's will, they must of necessity, also be uncreated by the same will. Thus does each person learn the folly of willful pride as compared to the peaceful joy prepared for us within the *Will* of our Father."

Jesus was silent and all knew he had finished. But there was none who needed more. The door to the kingdom of heaven had been plainly shown. And no longer need they fear a power of evil beyond their control.

Mary's entire being tingled. She remembered the day

on her roof in Nazareth when suddenly she was freed from resentment toward Zaele, thereby finding the first peace she had every known. Her peace had come when the voice from the sun told her to judge Zaele no longer. And now this voice, so much like the other voice, was explaining to all how they too could find this heavenly peace by not judging others.

"How wonderful!" she heard Elizabeth murmur at her side. "And how simple to understand."

"Yes," Mary answered, her vice hushed with wonder, "the kingdom of heaven is truly at hand. We need but have heart to feel and eyes to see its presence."

CHAPTER 21

For three years, Jesus and his disciples ministered to the people of Palestine. Mary and young Elizabeth became inseparable and often they followed Jesus and Peter as they moved from place to place. Mary saw many miraculous things performed. The sick were made whole. The blind to see. The lame to walk. And, on several occasions, the dead restored to life.

Once, after a bedridden woman was cured of her illness by merely touching the hem of Jesus' robe, Mary, who was walking far back in the procession, remembered the crippled young man in Hebron whose deformity she had caused to disappear. The voice of the sun then told her that many of humankind's physical infirmities carried with them a divine purpose.

As Mary pondered thusly, Jesus was suddenly walking beside her and he spoke directly into her thoughts. "That is true," he said, in answer to the question she was considering. "But it is also true that only where there has been faith have I made anyone whole. Those who are capable of having faith in my ability to administer the powers of God have become awakened and, therefore, need no longer their physical handicaps."

Jesus then disappeared from her side as quickly as he had appeared. Standing on tiptoe, Mary could see his beautiful head among the leaders of the procession and wondered if he had really left his position to dispel the question in her mind.

One day when Mary was living in her home in Jerusalem, Peter came to see her. She could see he was deeply disturbed as they chatted of many things. Finally, with a great sigh he turned his clear, simple eyes to hers and said, "Herod, on his birthday, made a supper to his lords, high captains, and chief landholders of Galilee. During the supper, Salome, daughter of Herodias, danced and so pleased Herod that he said, 'Ask of me whatsoever you will and I will give it unto the half of my kingdom.'

"Salome questioned Herodias, her mother, what she should ask. Our John, the Master's harbinger, was in Herod's prison because he had accused Herod of unlawfully taking unto himself Herodias, his brother's wife. Herodias, recognizing her opportunity to avenge herself against John, told her daughter to ask that the head of John the Baptist be brought forth upon a charger."

Peter paused, a deep sigh shook his tremendous frame, then he continued with averted eyes. "The king was reluctant, but he had made an oath, so he immediately sent an executioner who beheaded John in the prison and brought back upon a charger his head and placed it before the damsel. Salome fearfully directed him to take it to her mother.

Peter turned his eyes on Mary again. This time she read in them even greater pain and anxiety. She knew that the real cause of his distress was now about to be revealed.

"After this happened to John," Peter began with difficulty, "our Master Jesus told us that he himself must also suffer many things and would be rejected by the elders, priests, and scribes." Peter paused and wet his lips. With obvious effort he continued. "Then the Master said that he,

too, would be killed – and after three days, would rise
again!"

Peter groaned as he rested his massive head in his
hands. "I doubted him," he moaned, "for I could not
believe it. I told him that with a sweep of his hand he
could crumble the temple to earth."

"And what did he say?" Mary heard herself question
anxiously.

"He rebuked me," Peter replied woefully, "and said,
'you savor not the things of God, but the things that be of
humankind.'"

Both Mary and Peter were crushed beneath a weighty
silence. The fact that Jesus was to meet a fate similar to
John's so staggered Mary's mind that she was for a time
unconscious of her own existence. Then within her memory a thought began to stir. A phrase Peter had uttered was
repeating itself in the recesses of her mind. Clearer and
more emphatic it grew until her reason became vibrantly
alert to its significance.

"And after three days rise again!" Jesus had said that to
them. There was much Jesus said to his disciples that they
comprehended not. To rise from death after three days was
but another teaching that was beyond their understanding.
To be killed by the priests they did understand.

Since she was a maiden of fourteen, facing the rising
sun from her private sanctuary on the balustrade of the
temple, she had been waiting and listening for just this
evidence; evidence that Jesus would fulfill the mission of
the sun and demonstrate that humankind holds dominion
over the death it feared. And now, when the long-awaited
evidence had come, she recognized it not because it came

hand-in-hand with the distracting dragon humanity had made of death.

"How else could he demonstrate over death except that he die?" demanded her heart joyfully. Mary was relieved instantly. "Peter!" she exclaimed. "Peter!"

Roused from his miserable lethargy, he raised his head to Mary and stared incredulously at her smiling face. "Listen to me, Peter!" Mary urged, tugging at his sleeve. "Did not Jesus say that on the third day he would rise again?"

Automatically, Peter nodded his head.

"Don't you see what that means?" she exclaimed, looking deeply into his eyes. "Jesus told you he would be killed and then rise again. He is to bring himself back from the grave. You are not to lose your Master. If the grave cannot separate you from him, then you will be together forever. Think, Peter, think! Don't you see what this means to you and to all humankind? Has he not told you over and over, that what he does, you and all other people can do also!"

Slowly, Peter rose to his feet. As the truth of Mary's words illuminated his face, it was beautiful to behold. She watched in silence as his simple, direct mind assimilated the meaning of her words. Gradually, his eyes, staring into space, began to glow with wonder. "It is true!" he muttered dazedly. "It is true!"

As if in a trance, he turned and moved toward the door. Mary rose and walked with him. In a columned hallway they met Elizabeth where she waited to see Peter when his talk with Mary was finished. Rushing forward, she happily clasped his powerful arms, turning up to him a face aglow with love.

A smile flickered at the corners of Peter's lips. Clumsily putting an arm around her shoulders, he murmured, "Elizabeth! How happy I am to see you." He was yet too dazed to be completely aware of his actions. With no further word, Peter released Elizabeth and continued his trance-like tread through the doorway. Mary and Elizabeth watched him until he disappeared into the moving throngs beneath the brilliant sunlight.

In the days that followed, Elizabeth occupied herself continually with whatever activity she could find. Gradually, she assumed the responsibility of the requirements of Mary's home; and Mary, knowing her need for absorbing action, hindered her not.

One day she rushed breathlessly into Mary's chamber still carrying her market basket. With flushed cheeks and shining eyes, she related to Mary what she had seen. "I saw a crowd at the temple gate," she breathed. "I went to see what it meant and standing before the portion of the court used by the money-changers was Jesus. You should have seen him. He was wonderful! For a long time, he just stood and stared at them. His face was calm but his eyes were like lightning. Then slowly and deliberately, he took the cord from about his waist and attached it to his staff."

Elizabeth paused for a breath. "And then with the staff in his hand, he moved in upon the money-changers and began to lash them with the cord. Methodically and with no display of passion, he lashed them until all fell. So overcome were they by his manner that many left their money upon the changing tables. One, who seemed the wealthiest, was the last to go and before he went demanded of Jesus by what authority he did act. Jesus replied, 'It is written that my Father's house shall be a house of prayer and you have made it a den of thieves!"

Mary thrilled with Elizabeth's story. "He broke the lease agreement for that portion of the temple!" she exclaimed with approval.

"Lease?" Elizabeth questioned.

"Yes!" Mary explained. "The land upon which stands the temple belongs to Jesus as Prince of the House of David. When the land was leased by our fathers, it was written it should be used for a house of prayer. According to the law, if the land is used for other purposes than written in the lease, and if the owner approves not the purposes, he can break the lease by attaching his cord to his staff and whipping the offender off the land."

"How wonderful!" Elizabeth exclaimed. "But that is not all. He then went into the inner court where the rite of sacrifice was being performed. And I followed...."

Mary could hardly contain herself. "Tell me – hurry child! Tell me!" she pleaded.

"Many people were there and many lambs and doves had been killed and burned. Jesus did not stop until he reached the altar base. Then raising his arm and pointing above to the priest, he said in a loud voice, 'You people of Israel, know you not that your heavenly Father turns away his face from such cruel destruction of his beloved creatures?'"

"You should have heard the silence," Elizabeth interpolated, "and see the fear crawl across the face of the priest performing the rite."

"Hasten! Tell me all!" Mary begged. "What more did Jesus say?"

"Still pointing at the priest, he said, 'You need not this wanton butcher to receive your Father's blessings. To appeal through such a bloody mediator is but to withhold from yourselves your good. Think you that your Father God has need of Caesar's gold? The true altar of God is your heart. Destroy within its fire your anger, greed, lust, and fear and you will receive direct from God the blessings prepared for you., And then he disappeared," Elizabeth announced solemnly.

For a moment, Mary was silent, reviewing Elizabeth's story. Then she asked. "Did you tarry? What effect did his words leave on the people?"

"Many left. Some demanded back their money from the priest. Others shouted angry accusations. If the priest had not retired there would probably have been a riot."

Tears filled Mary's eyes. "Blessed Joseph and Zacharias!" she murmured. "If only they too could have seen this day, the fulfillment of that in which Joseph believed and for which Zacharias gave his life: the abolishment of animal sacrifice!"

The next morning Mary was weaving in the court of her house. She planned to make a waist for Elizabeth and wanted to finish the cloth before the day grew warm. A servant escorted a fully veiled woman into her presence and departed.

"May I be seated?" the caller asked, indicating a bench nearby.

Graciously, Mary nodded her head, curious about the familiarity of the woman's voice. When the visitor had seated herself, she removed her veils. It was Zaele! But what a changed Zaele. Her voluptuous beauty, which in

her youth was blatant and proud, now was reposed with a
delicate dignity and her once arrogant eyes were soft and
gentle with an arresting quality of charm. Mary was
delighted.

"Zaele!" she exclaimed, pulling her from the bench to
her feet and embracing her. Zaele's arms trembled as she
returned the embrace. Anxiously, she asked, "Do you
remember when I reported you to the tribunal and Ananias
attempted to have you disgraced?"

"Yes," Mary answered gently, drawing Zaele to the
bench beside her, "but that was only as an incident in our
childhood. Certainly not as anything yet to cause you concern."

A faint smile brightened Zaele's dark eyes as she spoke
and Mary could see in them genuine affection. "I know
that in your heart bitterness cannot live. But for years, I
have been chastised by the thought of what this deed
might have caused if Halhul had not been alive." Zaele
paused, her manner profoundly serious. "What Ananias
failed to accomplish when he tried to disgrace you, he
plans now to achieve by destroying the son you bore!"

Mary clutched the cool marble bench, but did not inter-
rupt. "After you made it possible for me to return to the
temple," Zaele continued, "and my understanding grew,
the meaning of Halhul's words when he accused Ananias
became very clear. I have seen his prophecy fulfilled.
After Halhul's death, I watched in secret the changing
methods of the temple. Ananias and his priests have but
one desire: to obtain the people's shekels so they may
spend them in riotous living outside the temple.

"Yesterday, after your Jesus endangered their most
profitable source of wealth, the rite of animal sacrifice,

they became exceedingly angry and excited. I hid and listened. They determine to dispose of him immediately.
They departed to the palace of Caiaphas, one of the high
priests, to discuss ways to dispose of Jesus. A cousin of
mine is a servant in Caiaphas' palace. From her, I learned
of the priests' debauchery, for much of it took place there.
I followed them to the palace and my cousin placed me
where I could hear their words."

Mary thrilled at Zaele's daring resourcefulness.

"In the meeting," Zaele continued, "besides the
Sadducees, there were also Pharisees, lawyers, and scribes.
All these obtain wealth by distorting truth before the people's eyes. And if your Jesus should sufficiently expose
them to the people they would lose their source of wealth
and also be in danger for their lives.

"I heard them plot. It was their plan to trick Jesus into
being guilty both of contempt for Caesar's laws and blasphemy according to Jewish laws. A Pharisee was chosen to
publicly question him concerning the payment of tribute
money. A Sadducee was chosen to attempt to confuse him
on the subject of resurrection, and a lawyer was named to
question him on the greatest of the commandments.

"Other men were chosen to go among the people with
money to buy those who would bear false witness and
those who would raise a cry of blasphemy and treason at
given signals.

"Caiaphas said his arrests must be made in secret, when
the multitudes were not near, else the common people
might stand forth in his defense. Ananias then told that the
twelve with Jesus went each day to pray in secret and if
their trysting place were found, then they could seize him
without the knowledge of the people.

"Then he added that he knew one of the twelve who did worship wealth, Judas by name, who for a sum, he believed, would lead him to the secret place. And Caiaphas said if Ananias would bribe this Judas to aid in seizing Jesus, the others would pay to Ananias thirty silver pieces. Ananias agreed."

Mary trembled. "Their plans are thorough," she managed to say.

"But now that they are known cannot he be saved?" Zaele inquired with desperate hope.

"That I do not know. I do not know that to be saved is in his plan. But this I will do. I will try to bear to him your message, for which I am deeply grateful."

Zaele nodded her head in humble acknowledgment.

Mary took her hand. "And Zaele," she added tenderly, "let this deed performed by you in behalf of me and the protection of Jesus free you forever of self-condemnation." Mary looked deeply into her eyes and repeated, "This you must do, beloved one, for it is just as unholy not to forgive ourselves as it is not to forgive others."

CHAPTER 22

When Zaele departed, Mary went to her favorite place of solitude on the roof. She felt the need of special spiritual strength to meet the coming events revealed by Zaele. She hardly seated herself when she heard footsteps ascending the stairs to the roof. It was Jesus! As he slowly approached Mary, he was directly between her and the sun, which made it appear as if he was walking toward her directly from the sun.

He sat beside her in silence for a moment, then tenderly took her hand in his. When he spoke, it seemed to Mary that his tone had never been so gentle and loving. "Remember when I first spoke to you from the sun?"

Mary nodded. Jesus continued. "Soon my earthly mission will be completed and I want to express my gratitude to you for making it possible."

Mary was too stirred to speak. All she could do was put her lips to his hand. Jesus raised her face and smiled reassuringly into her eyes. "Remember when the angel appeared in your room and announced that I would be born to you?" In reverence, Mary nodded again. "And the light came into the room, formed itself into a golden cone and entered your body?"

Mary closed her eyes with awe as she remembered. Jesus continued, "That particular light of the Holy Spirit has a special work to perform for humanity. It entered your body so that it could be infused into my earthly body.

And now the time has come for it to be released so that it can begin its work."

"What is its work?"

"It is to awaken humanity's soul from within. Before a seed can bear its fruit, it must be helped from the inside as well as the outside. Its growth is not only pulled upward by the outside sun, but it is also pushed upward by the tiny image of the fruit living in the seed.

"It is this inside 'image and likeness' that shall be awakened and pushed upward by my released light. This is its work ... to hover above the earth, as a loving mother, inspiring the image of God within every human to awaken and unfold itself."

Mary trembled with dread as she forced herself to ask, "How will this holy light be released?"

For a long moment, his only answer was to look upon her face, his eyes aglow with indescribable tenderness for what he knew his answer would do to her. Very gently, he said, "Since it is blended with my blood, it can only be released through the spilling of my blood."

A heart-rending sob escaped Mary's lips. She dropped her face into his lap and wept. Jesus' eyes glistened with tears of grief for her grief as he gently soothed her trembling shoulders.

Finally, Mary was able to speak. "I thought I was more prepared. Isn't there any other way?"

"Not if my mission is to be complete. So, little mother, let us rejoice that through the spilling of my blood, the blood you first built for me, will be released as a divine activity, which to the world will be its Savior. All will eventually respond to its constant knocking, the constant knocking at the door of their heart."

Mary lifted her face. It was now radiant with new awe. Jesus smiled at what he saw and said, "After I go away, there will be much confusion. I shall depend upon you to bring comfort to my disciples, to reveal certain truths to them that they are unable to understand while I am still with them."

Mary was stricken by such responsibility. "Will I be able to do such things?"

"I will always be with you. Also this light, which together we brought into the world, will comfort you with strength and wisdom when they are needed."

Mary bowed her head in holy humility. With a loving finality in his voice, Jesus said, "When your work is finished here, little mother, we will again be together in our service to all humankind."

When Mary, escorted by John the Beloved, made her way through the throng to the Mount of Golgotha, Jesus was already on the cross. On either side of him was a cross, occupied by a thief. At his feet, soldiers cast lots for his garments. With her heart in her eyes, Mary watched Jesus look down at the people who were so absorbed in their different feelings and actions. He lifted pain-racked eyes to heaven and said, "Forgive them, Father, for they know not what they do."

Then he looked down at Mary and John. Speaking directly to Mary, but indicating John with his eyes, he said, "Woman, behold thy son!"

Then speaking directly to John and indicating Mary with his eyes, he said, "Behold thy mother!"

John nodded his head understandingly, then protectively placed his arm about Mary's shoulders. A comforted smile tugged at the corners of Jesus' lips. Then he raised his head and gazed into the sun. In triumphant tones, he proclaimed, "My God, my God, how Thou has glorified me!"

The words were in Aramaic and many misunderstood their meaning.

His eyes closed and his head dropped to his chest. A soldier approached with a spear and pierced his side. As the gushing blood struck the air, it instantly became a blinding light, flashing and reflecting like lightning throughout the entire area. The light was so bright that it hid the sun and the earth, seemingly darkened, trembled. Many cries of fear and awe were heard.

Mary stared at the light with wonder in her eyes. "How glorious! How glorious is the light!" she exclaimed.

John was bewildered. "Light? I see no light! Only darkness!"

"The light is so bright, it darkens the sun."

Mary turned and looked around at Jerusalem and the surrounding area. The light reached to the horizon in every direction. As she watched, it seemed to nestle down closer and closer to the earth, becoming less bright as it became absorbed into the earth's atmosphere.

As the sunlight returned to normal, the people began to lose their fear. Mary looked deeply into John's awe-struck eyes, staring questioningly at her, and tried to explain. "Jesus told me the holy light would be released through his spilled blood … but not that it would darken the sun and shake the earth!"

John nodded, trying to understand. Mary raised her

gaze to Jesus' lifeless form. In reverent tones, she murmured confidently, "Now he will prove that the death humanity fears does not exist!"

The disciples gathered for a second time at Mary's home. They were still in varying states of bewilderment and excitement. Thomas took John by the shoulder and demanded, "Tell me again what has happened!"

Patiently, John replied. "We saw the empty sepulcher from which he had risen. Then when we met here, Jesus suddenly stood in our midst. He tried to reassure us. He told us to be at peace and that our real work would now begin. His words were 'As my Father sent me to teach you, I now send you to teach others.'"

Thomas was far from satisfied. "Except that I thrust my hand into his side, I still will not believe!"

Suddenly, as before, Jesus appeared in their midst. With a loving smile, he moved to the astonished Thomas and said, "Reach forth your hand and thrust it into my side."

Thomas did as he was told, instantly overcome with wonder. He reverently exclaimed, "My Lord! My Lord!"

With gentle understanding, Jesus said, "Thomas, because you have seen me, you believe. Blessed are they that do not see and yet believe."

Jesus' countenance became radiant with the holy love he felt as he looked slowly from on to the other. Then for a long moment, he gazed deeply into Mary's eyes. Very tenderly, he said, "When special wisdom you need, come to her. For she IS love, and love and wisdom are the same."

Then as suddenly as he appeared, he was gone. The faces of those in the room reflected the awe and inspiration with which they reacted to the divine responsibility which was now theirs.

CHAPTER 23

Mary and John were silent with their own thoughts as they ate together the next morning. Finally, John said, "In my mind I continue to see the others, each going forth in a different direction to do his work. Some I see walking, some on camels, some on boats, but in each face I see purposeful zeal and in each heart I feel the joy of unconquerable courage."

For a long moment, Mary looked at John, a quiet question in her eyes. Gently, she asked, "Do you wish you were one of them?"

John was quick to reply. "We were told that my life is to be with you ... and I am happy and proud that it is!" He avoided Mary's gaze for a moment, then asked, "Exactly, what is our work to be?"

"There is need of a place where those who hunger to know of the life, the love and light of Jesus can come. Here in his home shall be the place; and feeding the hungry shall be our work."

Her answer caused John's face to glow with joy.

Within a few weeks, the daily meetings in Mary's home had begun. When those who attended came from a long distance, they were provided with rooms and meals and made to feel as guests in every way. The meetings were conducted by both John and Mary, sometimes together, sometimes separately. But in either case, great was the comfort, peace, and joy that came from the love and wisdom of their ministry.

One day John approached Mary who was resting on the roof and said, "Remember Arioch, the shepherd to whom the angels proclaimed Jesus' birth?"

Mary nodded. "His grandson, Esek, is here on a litter," John continued. "He is now a leader of the Zealots and was wounded while attacking Roman soldiers in the wilderness. His followers, who brought him, say his legs and feet are paralyzed from a wound in his back ... they ask that you heal him."

Mary did not answer at once. Then very thoughtfully, she said, "I was once instrumental in healing a young man who had secretly coveted his brother's wife. With his healed body, he killed his brother and abducted the wife. Since our physical body is the garden provided for the growth of our soul, whatever changes occur in this garden either increase or decrease our earthly challenges, and it is our reaction to these challenges that determines whether or not we grow."

John nodded understandingly. In an effort to be helpful, he said, "Did not Jesus heal many bodies?"

"Yes, he did. But it seems his healings were always for and from the soul. Remember how frequently he stated, 'Your faith has made you whole.' or 'It is done to you as you believe it will be done unto you.'? Faith and belief are soul qualities."

"Since the purpose of earthly experience is the growth of our soul, shouldn't there be a way to reach through the body and quicken the soul? How great such a blessing would be! For would this not accelerate the very purpose of our life?" John said.

"I will ponder and pray concerning your words. Tell Esek's friends I cannot give them my answer now, but soon I will."

John gently closed the door behind him. Mary rose and walked slowly and thoughtfully about the room, stopping at the window and staring searchingly upward toward the mid-day sun. Aloud, she asked with deep sincerity, "How can I heal this man in both body and soul?"

Mary dropped to her knees in reverence as she heard a voice. "I am Archangel Michael come to answer your sincere question. Within the eternal heart of every individual flickers a tiny flame that is the body of his soul. As the intensity of this flame increases, its radiation reforms the physical, emotional, and mental bodies closer and closer to their inherent perfection. Therefore, the growth of a person's soul *can* be increased. It is done by the quickening of this flame."

"How can this flame be quickened?"

"By the vibrations of thought, feeling, or sound. If the soul cannot be reached by the thought of wisdom or the feeling of love, then it may be quickened by the sound of music."

"What kind of music?" Mary's voice sounded pleased with this idea.

"Both instrumental and of the human voice."

"But there are great differences in music, as well as in human voices."

"It is this necessary difference that can heal both body and soul."

Mary's next question revealed her perplexity. "And

how can this necessary difference be acquired?"

"It is the result of angels blending their vibratory sounds with that of the human."

"How wonderful," Mary murmured. "May one cause the angels somehow to provide this necessary blend?"

"Yes, Mary," the resonant voice of the great archangel replied. "All they need is your sincere invitation."

"How will I know my invitation is sufficiently sincere?"

"You will hear in your voice a newness of tone and range, also an additional harmony, richness, and beauty."

Eager to learn more, Mary asked, "Is the particular song important? Will I continue to sing the Psalms, the Songs of David?"

"Yes and no. The words of a song are not as important as the quality of vibration. That is, the color and hue of the tone. Therefore, the words you use may be completely new to you, may come from a pre-historic language or may even be formed for the first time for a particular need."

"What is a particular need?"

"I have assigned three special angels to help you. They will know the particular areas in which an individual needs to be helped and the particular tone-color necessary to heal those areas, both in body and soul. In the coming age, music will be used to overcome humanity's reluctance to grow. Sensitivity to beauty and truth in all forms will be quickened. This manner of increasing the present rate of human evolution is a decision that comes straight from the heart of the Creator's love for creation."

"It is a great and glorious gift," Mary said. Feeling the keen responsibility placed upon her, she asked very seriously, "How, oh, how will I know what to sing and what music to play?"

Michael replied gently and reassuringly, "When you invite the angels to help you, they will inspire you so strongly that you will do it automatically ... and when it is needed, they will sing with you ... adding their vibration to yours so that the healing is assured."

"How wonderful! How wonderful!"

The next day, Mary told John to have Esek brought to the meeting. His followers carried in the litter and sat on the floor around it. Mary began to strum the lyre with her fingers and to softly sing. As her singing grew stronger, it became so different that the regular group not only noticed, they were emotionally moved by it. It was a strange melody in a strange language.

Mary was not only awed by the stirring, heavenly, thrilling, and subtly powerful sounds coming from her voice, but she also sensed the holy sweetness of the presence of the angels. This brought to her heart a hitherto unfelt quality of joyous fulfillment.

As the music became more forceful in its purpose, Esek grew tense. He clenched his fist as though in resistance to something unfamiliar occurring within him. Then he began to relax. His fists slowly opened. His fingers reached forth as though to receive something desired in spite of himself.

One of the followers pressed Esek's arm to get his attention. When he did, he pointed to Esek's feet. His toes were wiggling and his legs were twisting from side to side.

Esek rapidly regained use of his legs. He and his followers remained in Mary's home awaiting his ability to travel. During that time, John and Esek had many talks from which blossomed a meaningful friendship. However, Esek's followers grew restless and impatient to resume their attacks upon Roman soldiers patrolling the wilderness.

One morning as Mary opened the door to her room to descend the stairs, she heard Esek speaking with his men in the inner court. The men said that now that Esek could travel, they needed to return to their work of avenging their God against the Romans. Mary's whole being thrilled with the words that came from Esek. "I no longer feel it right to kill individual soldiers. It does not serve our purpose. They are so many and we are so few. There has to be another way to establish our domain. If you, my friends, feel you must continue, it will have to be without me."

Mary's heart sang. "Both his body and his soul are healed!" she whispered to herself.

She listened further. There was a long silence below. Then came the strained voices of Esek's friends bidding him farewell. Mary went back into her room, knelt beside her bed and said aloud, "I want to express my deepest gratitude to the angels now helping me in my ministry and ask that I be a more and more effective instrument of their holy powers and purposes."

John and Esek stood together at the outer court of Mary's home watching people coming and going from inside the house where Mary was conducting a healing activity. John said, "Ever since she healed you, Esek, more and more people have been healed and more and more people come to be healed."

There was a new light of quiet peace in Esek's eyes and

in his voice. "It is difficult to believe the change in me. All I now want is to help her to help others."

"Her life has changed, too. She now has a new fulfillment. A new joy in her work. I don't know what your coming here had to do with it, but I am very grateful."

John approached Mary on the roof. "Esek is leaving," he said, "and asked to speak with you."

Mary was pleased. "Show him up here."

John went to the head of the stairs and motioned for Esek to come up. Mary greeted him pleasantly. "Come, sit beside me."

John started to descend the stairs. "Could John stay with us?" Esek asked.

Mary smiled and nodded, indicating a chair. For a moment, Esek stared with wonder at Mary. In a respectful tone, he added, "I wanted to thank you." Then, hesitantly, he added, "And I wanted to ask you a question."

"I hope I can answer it for you."

"No longer do I want to fight the Romans ... or anyone else. But how are we to obtain the promised freedom from our enemies? What about the covenant of God with the seed of Abraham? What about his promise to give us the land between the Nile and the Euphrates as our everlasting possession? How and when is this covenant to be fulfilled? When is this everlasting possession to begin?"

Mary's gaze moved pensively across the sky. She spoke quietly. "When we understand that the covenant is with individuals, all individuals, regardless of their nationality, we will know that it is already begun, already fulfilled."

"What do you mean?"

"You know, as I do, that Moses wrote those truths in allegory and symbolism. The Nile River has always symbolized the 'substance of life' and the Euphrates means 'that which makes fruitful.' So the 'promised land' between the rivers is an everlasting fruitful life for the individual who keeps his or her part of the covenant."

Esek was puzzled and thoughtful as he said, "Then why is not our life fruitful?"

"It must be because we have not kept our part of the covenant."

"But what is our part?" Esek persisted.

"Abram's name was not changed to 'Abraham' until after he became established in faith. Thus, God's covenant is with a person's faith. By the 'seed of Abraham,' Moses meant by the 'faith of the individual.'"

Both were silent a moment. Then Mary continued. "Which do most individuals feel the strongest: hate for our enemy or faith in God?"

Esek became deeply thoughtful. Slowly, he answered. "Before I came here, it was hate for our enemy."

Mary's voice became very quiet and authoritative. "This particular covenant of God with humanity was proclaimed on another occasion and that occasion was to your own grandfather the night Jesus was born. You must have heard him tell of the appearance of the angels while he and the others were tending their flocks."

Esek became excited, "I was there! I remember it! It was my fifth birthday and grandfather had promised to take me with him on my fifth birthday and let me spend the night."

Mary smiled at Esek's obvious joy, as she said, "Do you remember that the angels spoke of peace and goodwill?"

"Yes!"

"Well, peace depends upon goodwill. We cannot have one without the other. Peace on earth comes to persons of goodwill. Goodwill is not just a feeling or an attitude. It is a law or principle, just as a covenant is a law or principle."

Esek's sudden insight filled him with new enthusiasm. He jumped to his feet and proclaimed, "Only when an individual has striven within until he or she embodies love of God more than hatred of imagined enemies can God fulfill the covenant. Only when one wills for others the same good as for self can there be peace on earth!"

Esek struggled to contain his excitement so as to properly take his leave. His eyes were aglow with fervent gratitude as he spoke. "How wondrously you have answered my question, a question with which I have long struggled! Now I know how the kingdom is to be established! Now I know how the covenant is to be fulfilled. Now I know that humanity's most powerful weapon is the freedom to think what he will in his heart."

He turned to John who was beaming at the transformation in his friend and proclaimed, "Now I can fight the real enemy, the enemy of humanity's ignorance of its own true nature."

Esek enthusiastically embraced John, took one more adoring glance at Mary, then strode rapidly down the steps on his way to do battle with the outside world – now armed with the sword and the shield of his new understanding!

CHAPTER 24

Mary and John had ministered together for twenty years when on a certain day from far and near, the apostles arrived. No messenger had been sent. They just came. Time had dealt differently with each, but beneath the embers of age still glowed their dedication. On that same day, Zaele also arrived.

John acted as host. Shortly after their arrival, Mark, Philip, and James approached John. Mark said, "We were discussing how we happened to come here at the same time from different lands. I was in Ethiopia, James in Arabia, and Philip in India."

Philip added, "We all had a similar experience. Each of us felt an urge to come to Mary, an urge so strong it would not be denied."

James spoke excitedly. "Yes! We were led of the Spirit!" He gestured to the other apostles talking together and continued. "They all had the same feeling! John, you are closest to Mary. Do you know why this has happened?"

"Yes," John replied. "She told me that her time has come but she cannot go on until she has answered questions that may have arisen in your hearts concerning your ministry."

The three were shocked and grieved. They were silently thoughtful for a moment. Then Mark said, "It is true. I am troubled by many questions."

Philip said, "So am I!"

James echoed, "And I."

That evening everyone gathered on the roof. It was a warm, clear night. The heaven was filled with stars. Mary was reclining upon cushions on her couch. With age, her features had become more classical, her eyes more wise and loving. The apostles and household members were around her. There was an atmosphere of deep reverence and awe, for all knew that Mary was dying.

Mark approached a little closer and gently said, "John told us you would answer our questions concerning our ministry."

Mary smiled. "That is my desire. Please proceed."

"There are many things that trouble my heart," Mark began. "The tears of the afflicted flow and they cry out that God's ways are not equal for all. I have no answer except empty words of faith, which the painful facts seem to deny."

Then Thomas spoke. "This question has deeply troubled me. If this life be an opportunity for spiritual fulfillment, then it should be given equally to everyone. But some are strong and healthy and others are weak and sickly. Some are poor, laboring by day and night, leaving no time for prayer and devotion. Their bodies are weary and underfed, their minds clouded and confused. In this condition, how can they be expected to hear and practice my ministry?"

James spoke next. "And what of the slave who is forced to lie and steal ... who spends his life as the tool of another's evil mind? Surely, the ways of God are not equal with the slave and the master."

Nathanael's voice was filled with compassion. "And what of those born blind and maimed or die in their cradles? Or through sudden misfortunes are condemned to lie on their backs for the rest of their life? Have all these an opportunity for spiritual growth that is equal to those who are born healthy and remain strong all their lives?"

Then Phillip asked, "What about the difference in the ability to learn? Some children seem to be born with as much knowledge as others are able to acquire in a lifetime."

Bartholomew spoke with a tinge of accusation. "If God rewards righteousness and punishes iniquity, then how is it that some are born criminals and some saints? Where is justice when the righteous suffer misfortune after misfortune and the wicked remain secure and safe?"

Then Andrew, with a plea for logic, asked, "Is it just that only we who were taught of the Lord Jesus should be saved while those who lived before his day should be lost, simply because they could not have known the Master?"

Finally, came Peter's question. "If God be just, how could he choose unto himself one nation above the others, giving salvation to it alone while the Gentile world lives and dies in ignorance?"

Peter gestured toward all his fellow apostles who had asked questions and, in an anguished tone, concluded, "Must our faith in what we have been taught always be in conflict with our reason?"

Mary gazed with loving understanding into the eyes of each. Then she spoke. "That which appears as an inequality is the result of the very law by which our God expresses love equally for everyone. But before it can be understood, we must realize that the Divine Plan is that man and woman be perfect, even as their Father in heaven is perfect ... perfect in soul, in mind, and in circumstance. And this requires more than just one opportunity, more than just one lifetime."

John said, "Tell us how the law of equality works."

Mary continued. "To respect or fear this law is the beginning of wisdom, and wisdom is the beginning of our perfection. The first wisdom is learning that what we do to others is done unto us and with what we judgment we judge, we are also judged. This is why Jesus said that the two greatest commandments are to love God and to love our neighbor as ourselves. Not for the sake of God or our neighbors, but because of the way this law works. And why does it work the way it does? Because when we suffer the same way we have caused others to suffer, we eventually become wise enough not to inflict suffering upon others. Thus the law is called the Law of Growth. Growth, through wisdom, toward our perfection."

John became very excited. "I see! I see!" he declared. "The Law is our schoolmaster. It disciplines us until we are willing to choose the wisdom of love."

With new hope, Peter asked, "Even though we now see more clearly, how can we make our people understand?"

"Blessed Peter," Mary replied. "If you will 'go up' in consciousness to an awareness of your God-self and speak to their God-selves, there will be a communication of such quickening that their vehicles of knowing will be instantly expanded with new wisdom."

Peter's hope increased. "How can I have faith that this higher communication with others can and does occur?"

Mary smiled and, with tenderness in her voice, explained, "There is but *one* Life, Peter. The Life of God. So this communication of yours is simply God as you and as your flock, talking to himself about his own perfection."

Peter now became excited. "I remember! At the Master's last discourse with us, he tried to explain this oneness, this unity, this God-in-all-as-all. I think he said it this way, 'I am in my Father and ye in me, and I in you.'"

Mary said to Peter, "Within this unity is contained the answer to yours and Andrew's first question, for everyone, regardless of time or place of birth, in some life and at some time, will be given the opportunity to know the truth of the wondrous nature of God's love. Furthermore, when a soul is given a new body, it is always provided the environment best suited for its particular growth."

There was a thrill-laden silence broken only by the sound of a rooster crowing in the distance announcing the approaching dawn. Then Zaele spoke and Mary's special love for her was so very obvious as she listened to her words. "What about the pitiful plight of women? Men make their sport of them and then cast them out to hunger and shame, to be considered less than a horse or dog, wile the man remains well spoken of in the synagogue?"

Into Mary's voice came a tone of celestial authority as she answered. "In every man there is the love and gentleness of a woman. In every woman, the wisdom and strength of man. Thus, in each sleeps the nature of the other. As that which sleeps awakens, each will express both love and wisdom. The purpose of the light that our Lord brought to earth is to do this awakening. Thus, the new stature of woman and the new nobility of man has already begun. And of its increase, there shall be no end!"

Suddenly, Mary's face began to glow in the pre-dawn darkness. There was a beautiful blue light all about her. She rose from her couch and stood erect. To the astonishment and awe of the others, her face and figure slowly dissolved into the appearance that was hers in her youth. There was the muted sound of a heavenly choir. Then very near and above them, the darkness parted like the curtain of a large stage revealing an area lit by this same beautiful blue light. The area was filled with a few people surrounded by many angels. Closest to the roof stood Jesus, then John the Harbinger, Elizabeth, Zacharias, Anna, Joachim, Joseph, and Halhul. Regardless of their former ages, each appeared to be in the prime of life. Those who were on the roof automatically rose to stare at those beyond the curtain.

Different generations and different positions were represented by those on the roof. Grandchildren, parents, grandparents, apostles and servants all staring upward with the same awe-struck reverent light in their eyes. Those above looked down with joy and loving understanding at those looking up at them. Two worlds, the visible and the invisible, sending love and devotion across the opened curtain that usually separated them.

Suddenly, above them all appeared the radiant majesty of the Archangel Michael! His arms reached forth a welcome as he said, "Hail Mary! Blessed among women! Now you shall do the things for which you have hungered: attend the birth of every child, heal the sick of body and soul, comfort the downtrodden, and bring forth the upliftment of womanhood throughout the world. To serve you in this work, I now place into your hands the mighty power of the heavenly hosts. Henceforth, you shall be called 'Queen of the Angels.'"

Slowly, Mary began to ascend. She turned and looked back at those she was leaving. She held out her ands and moved them back and forth in a blessing as she rose higher and higher. Jesus reached out his hand and drew her to his side. The heavenly choir pealed out in all its glory. The curtain slowly closed just as the tip of the rising sun appeared above the horizon. The rays of the newborn sun streaked up and across the heavens, transforming the hovering clouds into a cosmic cathedral of rapturous colors.

The heavenly choir swelled to the peak of its angelic ecstasy. The music seemed to be coming from inside this etheric cathedral as though it were part of a celestial service, a service whose purpose was to proclaim to the world the birth of a new age.

BIOGRAPHY

**Arnold Michael,
D.D., L.H.D.**

Arnold Michael, D.D., L.H.D., dedicated his life to furthering a better understanding between the East and West – the old world of awareness and the new world of action. Therefore, the themes of his books blend mysticism and new thought, contemplation with positive thinking, meditation with spiritual mind treatment.

Dr. Michael's background contributes authority to his ability to provide this blend. From 1952-1970, he was a Church of Religious Science Minister and the Minister Emeritus founder of the Sacramento Church of Religious Science. From 1979 until his 1987 transition, he was first a priest, then a bishop in the Church of Antioch. Throughout his life, he was considered one of the outstanding teachers, writers, ministers, and counselors of the expanding metaphysical New Thought Movement of the 20th Century.

In 1969, Arnold and his wife Kathryn (Kay) moved onto pine-forested land where the pine trees seemed to talk to him in their whisperings. Here, he established the

Church of the Talking Pines. Devoted to the Beloved Mother Mary, he began calling his work the Madonna Ministry. In 1981 he wrote these words, "I feel a keen urge to serve as an instrument to bring to human awareness the nature and evolutionary purpose of the feminine aspect of our Father-Mother God – referred to as *The Comforter, The Feminine, The Divine Mother, The Holy Ghost* – so that we may consciously and more deliberately cooperate with Its purpose."

His first novel, *Blessed Among Women*, drew many others to this work as Emissaries of the Divine Mother. In 1983, through his authority as a Church of Antioch bishop and the legally established status of the Church of the Talking Pines, Arnold began ordaining ministers in the Madonna Ministry. At this turning of an age, the ministers and bishops in this now international ministry are increasing in numbers and the ministry's message of service based on one's inner divine authority and commitment to peace, within and without, is spreading.

Kay Michael's reflection on her husband, Arnold, captures the essence of this highly evolved being. "To say that Arnold Michael was charismatic is somewhat understating his personality. When most people met him for the first time, they were impressed that they were in the presence of a *Presence*. Many later remarked to me, or to somebody else, that his blue eyes seemed to penetrate right into their soul; some said he had the eyes of an 'adept.' When he was asked a question of spiritual import, he often seemed to click into a higher consciousness and speak from a plane of *knowing*. These traits became more pronounced as he grew older until finally, during the last part of his life when he was an invalid, people would hear of him and come from far places, often bringing a gift, just to be at his bedside and to hear him talk and teach."

His legacy of divine love and truth lives on in his writings through *Discipline of Delight, Brothers of the Grape, Blessed Among Women, The Truth of Being* and twenty-five newsletter entitled: *Madonna Ministry.*

The Madona Ministry newsletter have this theme and statement running through them: *"The Way the Divine Mother gives birth to and nurtures our individual Christ Self."*

For information regarding Arnold Michael's works please contact Global Citizen Publishing. For information regarding the Madonna Ministry go to:

www.madonnaministry.org or
www.madonnaministry.net